FABULOUS CROCHETED PONCHOS

FABULOUS CROCHETED PONCHOS

Terry Taylor

LARK BOOKS

A Division of Sterling Publishing Co., Inc.
New York

Technical Editor: Karen Manthey
Art Director: Tom Metcalf
Cover Designer: Barbara Zaretsky
Assistant Editor: Nathalie Mornu
Associate Art Director: Shannon Yokeley
Editorial Assistance: Delores Gosnell
Photography: Stewart O'Shields
Illustrations: Orrin Lundgren
Hair and Makeup: Diane Chambers

Library of Congress Cataloging-in-Publication Data

Taylor, Terry, 1952-
  Fabulous crocheted ponchos : new styles, new looks, new yarns / Terry B.
Taylor.— 1st ed.
      p. cm.
  Includes index.
  ISBN 1-57990-722-9 (pbk.)
  1. Crocheting—Patterns. 2. Shawls. 3. Cloaks. I. Title.
TT825.T38 2005
746.43'40432—dc22

                    2005012850

10 9 8 7 6 5 4 3 2 1

First Edition

Published by Lark Books, A Division of
Sterling Publishing Co., Inc.
387 Park Avenue South, New York, N.Y. 10016

© 2005, Lark Books

Distributed in Canada by Sterling Publishing,
c/o Canadian Manda Group, 165 Dufferin Street
Toronto, Ontario, Canada M6K 3H6

Distributed in the U.K. by Guild of Master Craftsman Publications Ltd., Castle Place, 166 High Street, Lewes, East Sussex,
England BN7 1XU
Tel: (+ 44) 1273 477374, Fax: (+ 44) 1273 478606, e-mail: pubs@thegmcgroup.com, Web:www.gmcpublications.com

Distributed in Australia by Capricorn Link (Australia) Pty Ltd.,
P.O. Box 704, Windsor, NSW 2756 Australia

If you have questions or comments about this book, please contact:
Lark Books
67 Broadway
Asheville, NC 28801
(828) 253-0467

Manufactured in China

For information about custom editions, special sales, premium and corporate purchases, please contact
Sterling Special Sales Department at 800-805-5489 or specialsales@sterlingpub.com

contents

ponchos. ponchos? ponchos!

introduction

they're everywhere. And absolutely everyone seems to be wearing one. OK, maybe your brother-in-law isn't—but trendy, fashion-conscious teens and glittering screen stars are wearing them. So are magazine moguls and stylish moms with babes in arms—and grandmothers!

If you want to make a poncho that stands out from the crowd make one with crochet. Crochet is a versatile—and easy to learn—technique that's perfect for making ponchos. And you can crochet with any of those soft silks, bulky warm wools, fun-to-work-with ribbons, or any one of today's great yarns.

Do you yearn for warm ponchos to fend off autumn's chill? Choose soft-to-the-touch wool yarns and patterns with closely spaced stitches. Attach scarves to the necklines to saucily toss over your shoulder or wrap around your neck. Imitate the intricate structure of an Aran sweater with cables and bobbles that are made up of simple stitch combinations.

Do you crave a lacy poncho to dress up a little black dress? Crochet is perfect for creating skin-caressing, openwork lace effects with featherweight novelty yarns, or use bold color to give a Bohemian

twist to a lacy pattern. Crochet a delicate, form-fitting capelet with fine mohair, then top it off with a matching floral accent.

There are so many fabulous ponchos to make in this book, you'll need to start working on one right away to get them all done. We've grouped the ponchos by skill level, just in case it's been a while since you thought about crochet and you want to start with something simple. Once you've brushed up on your skills, you can move right on to any other pattern your heart desires.

If you're a beginner or need to refresh your memory about a certain stitch, refer to the crochet basics section that starts on page 105. It's a handy resource for crocheters of all levels.

Follow our designers' innovative patterns and yarn choices; then, if you want, select your own yarns to personalize the look—there's an easy way to do that and we'll tell you how. You can make a great-looking poncho that won't look exactly like a famous film star's, your great-grandmother's, or anyone else's for that matter!

The rich plum-blue of this poncho is accented with a lusciously soft cowl neck. If the wind blows fiercely, pull the generous neck up and over your head. It's a great look—with or without tassels.

AMORÉ • *Designed by Laura Gebhardt*

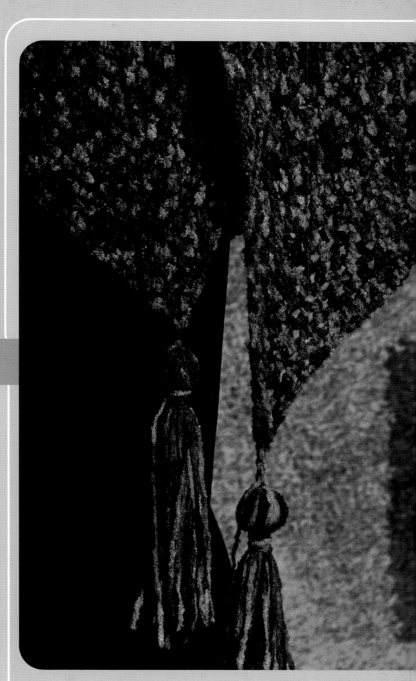

SKILL LEVEL: EASY

FINISHED MEASUREMENTS
One size fits most
Front: 44"/112cm
wide x 19"/48cm long.
Back: 44"/112cm
wide x 23.5"/60cm long.

YOU WILL NEED
Approx 1284yd/1174m
medium worsted
weight yarn
Hook: 5.5 mm/ I–9 or size
needed to
obtain gauge
Piece of cardboard or book
approximately 10"/25cm
across

STITCHES USED
Chain stitch (ch)
Half double crochet (hdc)
Single crochet (sc)
Slip stitch (sl st)

GAUGE
*Take time to check
your gauge.*
13 sts and 9 rows =
4"/10cm in hdc.

Back

Ch 145.

Row 1: Hdc in 5th ch from hk, *ch 1, sk next ch, hdc in next ch, rep from * across, turn (71 ch-1 sps/143 sts)

Row 2: Ch 2, hdc in next ch-1 sp, *ch 1, sk next hdc, hdc in next ch-1 sp, rep from * across to last st, hdc in 2nd ch of ch-4 beg ch in Row 1, turn (70 ch-1 sps/143 sts).

Row 3: Ch 3 (counts as beg hdc and ch 1), sk next hdc, hdc in next ch-1 sp, *ch 1, sk next hdc, hdc in next ch-1 sp, rep from * across to last 2 sts, ch 1, sk next hdc, hdc in top of beg ch 2, turn.

Row 4: Ch 2, hdc in next ch-1 sp, *ch 1, sk next hdc, hdc in next ch-1 sp, rep from * across to last st, hdc in 2nd ch of beg ch 3.

Rows 5–53: Rep Rows 3–4, ending with Row 3. Fasten off.

Front

Work as given for back until 38 rows are completed.

Shaping Neck and Left Shoulder

Row 39: Work in patt across 61 sts (30 ch-1 sps), turn, leaving rem sts unworked.

Row 40: Ch 1, hdc in next ch-1 sp (dec made); work in patt across.

Row 41: Work in patt across 59 sts (29 ch-1 sps), turn.

Row 42: Rep Row 40.

Row 43: Work in patt across (28 ch-1 sps). Fasten off.

Right Shoulder

Row 39: Sk next 10 ch-1 sps, rejoin yarn with sl st in next ch-1 sp. Ch 3, work in patt across, turn (30 ch-1 sps).

Row 40: Ch 2, work in pattern across, turn.

Row 41: Ch 2, hdc in next ch-1 sp (dec made), work in pattern across, turn (29 ch-1 sps).

Row 42: Rep Row 40.

Row 43: Rep Row 41 (28 ch-1 sps). Fasten off.

Assembly

Sew front to back across the shoulders.

Cowl Neck

Rnd 1: Join yarn with sl st in 1st free st at back neck after right shoulder seam, ch 2, hdc in each hdc and ch-1 sp across back neck (31 hdc), working in ends of rows, work 10 hdc evenly space down left shoulder, work 21 hdc evenly spaced across front neck, work 10 hdc evenly spaced up right shoulder. Join with sl st to top of beg ch 2 (72 hdc).

Rnd 2: Ch 2, hdc in each hdc around. Join with sl st to top of beg ch 2 (72 hdc).

Rep Row 2 until collar measures approx 13"/33cm from beg. Fasten off. Weave in ends.

Tassels (make 4)

Wrap yarn 30 times around a book or 6"/15cm piece ofcardboard. Carefully slip the wrapped yarn off of the form, holding it together. Wrap a length of yarn around the tassel tightly near the top. Secure the wrapping yarn. Thread a yarn needle with yarn and stitch the tassel to one corner. Trim the tassel as desired.

THIS PROJECT WAS CREATED WITH 6 skeins of TLC *Amore* in Plum Print (#3934), 80% acrylic/20% nylon, 4½ oz/128g = 214yd/196m

Caramel doesn't have to mean sticky! Oh no, this poncho is made with soft, warm yarns, and just a touch of metallic accent to make it dressy—and deliciously stylish.

CARAMEL PONCHO • *Designed by Robyn Kelly*

SKILL LEVEL: EASY

FINISHED MEASUREMENTS
One size fits most
Length: 45"/114cm from Back neck edge to bottom point
Width: 39"/99cm at widest point

YOU WILL NEED
765yd/689m bulky bouclé yarn (A)
164yd/150m worsted weight mohair yarn (B)
Hook: size 9mm/M–13 or size needed to obtain gauge
Eight 1"/2.5cm decorative buttons

Sewing needle and matching sewing thread

STITCHES USED

Chain stitch (ch)

Double crochet (dc)

Single crochet (sc)

Slip stitch (sl st)

SPECIAL STITCH TECHNIQUES

Extended single crochet (esc): Insert hook in next st, yo, draw yarn through st, yo, draw through 1 loop on hook, yo, draw

Extended single crochet decrease (esc2tog): (Insert hook in next st, yo, draw yarn through st, yo, draw through 1 loop on hook) twice, yo, draw through 3 loops on hook.

Decrease 2 extended single crochet (esc3tog): (Insert hook in next st, yo, draw yarn through st, yo, draw through 1 loop on hook) 3 times, yo, draw through 4 loops on hook.

GAUGE

Take time to check your gauge.

6 sts and 5 rows esc = 4"/10cm

Front

Starting at bottom point, with A, ch 2.

Row 1: Sc in 2nd ch from hook, turn (1 sc)

Row 2: Ch 1, 3 sc in sc, turn (3 sc)

Row 3: Ch 2, 2 esc in first sc, esc in next sc, 2 esc in last sc, turn (5 esc)

Row 4: Ch 2, esc in each esc across (5 esc).

Rows 5–7: Ch 2, 2 esc in first esc, esc in each esc across to last st, 2 esc in last esc (11 esc at end of last row).

Row 8: Rep Row 4 (11 esc).

Rows 9–11: Rep Row 5 (17 esc at end of last row). Fasten off A, join B.

Row 12: With B, ch 3, *sc in next st, dc in next st; rep from * across, turn (17 sts). Fasten off B, join A.

Rows 13–15: With A, rep Row 5 (23 esc at end of last row).

Row 16: Rep Row 4 (23 esc).

Row 17–19: Rep Row 5 (29 esc at end of last row). Fasten off A, join B.

Rows 20–35: Rep Rows 12–19 (twice) (53 esc at end of last row).

Rows 36–40: Rep Rows 12–16 (59 esc at end of last row).

Rows 41–43: Ch 2, esc2tog in first 2 sts, esc in each across to last 2 sts, esc2tog in last 2 sts (53 esc at end of last row). Fasten off A, join B.

Row 44: Rep row 12 (53 esc). Fasten off B, join A

Rows 45–51: Rep Row 41 (39 esc at end of last row).

Rows 52–67: Rep Rows 44-51 (twice) (23 esc at end of last row).

Rows 68–72: Rep Rows 44-48 (3 esc at end of last row).

Row 73: Ch 2, esc3tog in next 3 sts, turn (1 st). Fasten off.

Back

Work same as Front through Row 59 (25 sts).

Assembly

Place right sides of front and back facing, matching stitches across side edge.

Join A at end of Row 41 (first dec row), working through double thickness, sl st in each st across to last row of back. Fasten off. Rep on opposite side edge.

Bottom Trim

With RS facing, join 2 strands of B at one side seam on bottom edge of poncho.

Ch 1, sc around lower edge of poncho, working 3 sc in each point. Sl st in first sc to join. Fasten off.

Neck Trim

With RS facing, join 2 strands of B at one side seam on neck edge of poncho.

Ch 1, sc evenly around neck edge of poncho, working 3 sc in point. Sl st in first sc to join. Fasten off.

Finishing

Sew 4 buttons, evenly spaced across each side edge of poncho.

THIS PROJECT WAS CREATED WITH 3 skeins of Bernat's *Soft Bouclé* in Softest Straw (#26515), 98% acrylic/2% polyester, 5 oz/140g = 255yd/232m

2 skeins of Lion Brand *Moonlight Mohair* in Safari (#203), 35% mohair/30% acrylic/25% cotton/10% metallic polyester,1¾ oz/50g = 82yd/75m

This one's almost too cute for words. Surely you know some young miss (or perhaps you are one!) who'd look just, well, pretty in pink.

PRETTY IN PINK CAPELET • *Designed by Kalpna Kapoor*

SKILL LEVEL: INTERMEDIATE

FINISHED MEASUREMENTS
Women's size S/M.
Neck edge: 33½"/85cm in circumference.
Bottom edge: 42½"/ 108cm in circumference.
Length: 9"/23cm

YOU WILL NEED
Approx 274yd/250m light wosted weight yarn
Hook: 5 mm/H–8 or size needed to obtain gauge

STITCHES USED
Chain stitch (ch)
Double crochet (dc)
Slip stitch (sl st)

SPECIAL STITCH
Popcorn (pop): Work 5 dc in same st, drop loop from hook, insert hook from front to back in 1st of 5 dc, draw dropped loop through st.

GAUGE:
Take time to check your gauge.
20 sts and 8 rows = 4"/10cm in dc

PATTERN NOTES
Adjust the capelet to fit larger sizes by working a longer foundation chain. Work an even number of stitches to desired length for circumference around neck edge.

Pattern

Starting at neck edge, ch 126 (or an even number of sts to desired length) and, without twisting ch, close into a ring with 1 sl st in 1st ch.

Rnd 1: Ch 4 (counts as dc, ch 1), skip 1st 2 ch, *dc in next ch, ch 1, skip next ch; rep from * around. Sl st to 3rd ch of turning ch to join (63 ch-1 spaces).

Rnd 2: Ch 4 (counts as dc, ch 1), dc in 1st ch-1 space (inc made), ch 1, (dc, ch 1) in each dc around, sl st to 3rd ch of turning ch to join (64 ch-1 spaces).

Rnds 3–18: Rep Rnd 2, working one inc in diffeerent places in each rnd (80 ch-1 spaces at end of Rnd 18). Fasten off.

Flower

Ch 6 and close into a ring with 1 sl st in 1st ch.

Rnd 1 (RS): Ch 3 (counts as 1st dc of beg pop), 4 dc in ring, drop loop from hook, insert hook in top of turning ch, draw dropped loop through st (beg pop made), (Pop, ch 3) 6 times in ring, sl st in 3rd ch of turning ch to join (7 pops).

Rnd 2: Sl st in 1st ch–3 space, ch 3 (counts as 1st dc of beg pop), beg pop in 1st ch-3 space, ch 3, (pop, ch 3) in each ch-3 space around, sl st in 3rd ch of turning ch to join (7 pops).

Rnd 3: Sl st to center dc of 1st pop, ch 1, *sc in center dc of pop, ch 3, sc in next ch-3 space, ch 3; rep from * around, sl st in 1st sc to join (14 ch-3 spaces. Fasten off.

Finishing

With yarn needle and yarn, sew flower to top of capelet as desired. Sew pearl bead to center.

This Project Was Created With 2 balls of Plymouth *Wildflower D.K.* in Pink (#80), 51% cotton/49% acrylic, 1.75oz/50g = 137 yd/125m

The washed and faded hues of this poncho make it the perfect partner for your most faded (and treasured) blue jeans.

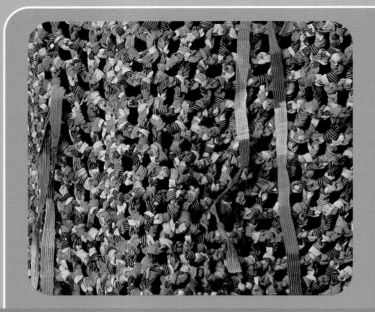

DANDY DENIM PONCHO   • *Designed by Marty Miller*

SKILL LEVEL: EASY

FINISHED MEASUREMENTS
One size fits most
Neck Opening: 11"/28cm circumference
Width: 52"/132cm at widest point of triangles
Length: 26"/66cm from neck edge to center front point

YOU WILL NEED
Approx 880yd/792m ribbon yarn
Hook: 6.5mm/K–10½ or size needed to obtain gauge

STITCHES USED
Chain st (ch)
Single crochet (sc)
Slip stitch (sl st)

GAUGE
Take time to check your gauge.

(Sc, ch 5) 4 times in pattern = 4"/10cm
7 rows in pattern = 4"/10cm

PATTERN NOTES
To begin this project, start crocheting the poncho from the center of the top, working down the sides of the triangle, turning every row. You can make the triangle as deep as you want from the long side to the opposite point.

There is no right side or wrong side to this poncho until it is assembled. When you start or end a skein, leave a 6-8"/15-20cm end. This will become the fringe on the body of the poncho.

You can alter the size of this poncho as desired by working more or fewer rows.

Front/Back (make 2)

Ch 5 and close into a ring with 1 sl st in first ch.

Row 1: Ch 5, sc in ring, ch 5, sc in ring, ch 2, dc in ring (counts as ch-5 loop), turn (3 ch-5 loops).

Row 2: Ch 5, sc in first ch-5 loop, ch 5, (sc, ch 5, sc) in next ch-5 sp (center loop made), ch 5, (sc, ch 2, dc) in last ch-5 loop, turn (5 ch-5 loops).

Row 3: Ch 5, sc in first ch-5 sp, ch 5, sc in next ch 5 loop, ch 5, (sc, ch 5, sc) in next ch-5 sp (center loop made), ch 5, sc in next ch-5 loop, ch 5, (sc, ch 2, dc) in last ch-5 loop, turn (7 ch-5 loops).

Rows 4–37: Ch 5, sc in first ch-5 sp, ch 5, (sc, ch 5) in each loop across to center loop, (sc, ch 5, sc) in center loop, ch 5, (sc, ch 5) in each loop across to last ch-5 loop, (sc, ch 2, dc) in last ch-5 loop, turn (75 ch-5 loops at end of Row 37). Do not fasten off. Do not weave in ends.

Joining Row: Place front and back together, with one ball of attached yarn on each side, matching sts all around. Place a marker at each end of center 11"/28cm across top edge of front and back. With attached yarn on right-hand side, ch 1, working through double thickness of front and back, work 3 sc in each sp across to marker. Do not fasten off. Turn poncho around. Working from other end with other ball of attached yarn, ch 1, working through double

thickness of front and back, work 3 sc in each sp across to marker. Do not fasten off.

Try poncho on to make sure neck opening is sufficient. Adjust opening as needed, keeping opening it centered. Fasten off one side, leaving a 6–8"/15–20cm fringe length.

Neck Edging

With rem attached ball of yarn, sc evenly around neck opening. Sl st in first sc to join. Fasten off.

Finishing

Joining Row designates right side of poncho. Bring all the fringe ends to the right side. If you want to add more fringe, cut 12-16"/30–41cm lengths of yarn and tie them on, using the center of the strand, at random places on the poncho.

This Project Was Created With

11 skeins of Crystal Palace Yarns *Deco Ribbon* in Jeans (#7237), 70% acrylic/30% nylon, 1¾oz/50g = 80yd/72m

Snuggling into a poncho of sheepskin sounds divine but would be all-too-heavy to wear. Create a pretty facsimile with suede-look yarn that's easy on the shoulders and will keep you almost as cozy.

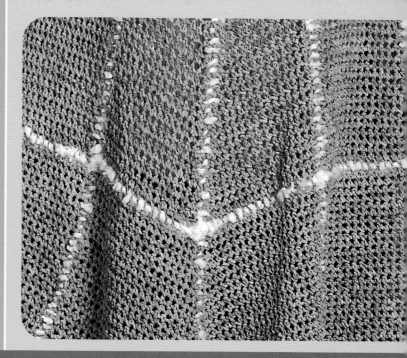

FAUX SHEEPSKIN PONCHO • *Designed by Marty Miller*

SKILL LEVEL: EASY

FINISHED MEASUREMENTS
One size fits most
Neck opening: 24"/61cm circumference
Bottom Width: 105"/267cm circumference
Length: 30"/76cm from neck to center front point

YOU WILL NEED
Approx 1200yd/1097m suede-look worsted weight yarn (A)
Approx 416yd/380m bulky weight bouclé yarn (B)
Hook: 10mm/N–15 or size needed to obtain gauge
Stitch markers
Yarn needle

STITCHES USED
Chain stitch (ch)
Single crochet (sc)
Slip stitch (sl st)

SPECIAL STITCH TECHNIQUES
Single crochet decrease (sc2tog): (Insert hook in next st, yo, draw yarn through st) twice, yo, draw yarn through 3 loops on hook.
Decrease 2 single crochet (sc3tog): (Insert hook in next st, yo, draw yarn through st) 3 times, yo, draw yarn through 4 loops on hook.

GAUGE
Take time to check your gauge.
10 sts and 11 rows sc = 4"/10cm

PATTERN NOTES
Each of the back and front pieces (Motifs A, B, C, and D, 1 and 2) have decreases only on one side. Place a marker on the side of the piece where you will be making your decreases. The top side pieces (Motif F) have decreases on both sides. You don't need to place a marker on these pieces. When joining new yarn, join at the end of a row. The even numbered rows are worked on the right side of each piece.

Motif A-1 (make 2)

With A, ch 35.

Row 1 (WS): Sc in 2nd ch from hook, sc in each ch across, turn (34 sc). Place a marker on this edge for dec side

Row 2 (RS): Ch 1, sc2tog in first 2 sts, sc in each sc across, turn (33 sc).

Row 3: Ch 1, sc in each sc across, turn (33 sc)

Row 4: Rep Row 2 (32 sc).

Rows 5–30: Rep Rows 3-4 (13 times) (19 sc at the end of Row 30). Fasten off

Motif A-2 (make 2)

Motif A-2 is the reverse shaping of Motif A-1.

With A, ch 35.

Row 1 (WS): Sc in 2nd ch from hook, sc in each ch across, turn (34 sc). Place a marker at beg of Row 1 for dec side.

Row 2 (RS): Ch 1, sc in each sc across to last 2 sts, sc2tog in last 2 sts, turn (33 sc).

Row 3: Ch 1, sc in each sc across, turn (33 sc).

Row 4: Rep Row 2 (32 sc).

Rows 5–30: Rep Rows 3–4 (13 times) (19 sc at the end of Row 30). Fasten off.

Motif B-1 (make 2)

With A, ch 20.

Row 1 (WS): Sc in 2nd ch from hook, sc in each ch across, turn (19 sc). Place a marker at beg of Row 1 for dec side.

Row 2 (RS): Ch 1, sc in each st across, turn (19 sc)

Row 3: Ch 1, sc2tog in first 2 sts, sc in each sc across, turn (18 sc).

Rows 4–5: Ch 1, sc in each st across, turn (18 sc).

Row 6: Ch 1, sc in each sc across to last 2 sts, sc2tog in last 2 sts, turn (17 sc).

Row 7: Ch 1, sc in each st across, turn (17 sc).

Row 8: Ch 1, sc in each sc across to last 2 sts, sc2tog in last 2 sts, turn (16 sc).

Rows 9–10: Ch 1, sc in each st across, turn (16 sc).

Row 11: Ch 1, sc2tog in first 2 sts, sc in each sc across, turn (15 sc).

Row 12: Ch 1, sc in each st across, turn (15 sc).

Row 13: Ch 1, sc2tog in first 2 sts, sc in each sc across, turn (14 sc).

Rows 14–15: Ch 1, sc in each st across, turn (14 sc).

Row 16: Ch 1, sc in each sc across to last 2 sts, sc2tog in last 2 sts, turn (13 sc).

Row 17: Ch 1, sc in each st across, turn (13 sc).

Row 18: Ch 1, sc in each sc across to last 2 sts, sc2tog in last 2 sts, turn (12 sc).

Rows 19–20: Ch 1, sc in each st across, turn (12 sc).

Row 21: Ch 1, sc2tog in first 2 sts, sc in each sc across, turn (11 sc).

Row 22: Ch 1, sc in each st across, turn (11 sc)

Rows 23–36: Rep Rows 21–22 (7 times) (4 sc at end of Row 36). Fasten off.

Motif B-2 (make 2)

Motif B-2 is the reverse shaping of Motif B-1)

With A, ch 20.

Row 1 (WS): Sc in 2nd ch from hook, sc in each ch across, turn (19 sc). Place a marker on this edge for dec side.

Row 2 (RS): Ch 1, sc in each st across, turn (19 sc).

Row 3: Ch 1, sc in each sc across to last 2 sts, sc2tog in last 2 sts, turn (18 sc).

Rows 4-5: Ch 1, sc in each st across, turn (18 sc).

Row 6: Ch 1, sc2tog in first 2 sts, sc in each sc across, turn (17 sc).

Row 7: Ch 1, sc in each st across, turn (17 sc).

Row 8: Ch 1, sc2tog in first 2 sts, sc in each sc across, turn (16 sc).

Rows 9–10: Ch 1, sc in each st across, turn (16 sc).

Row 11: Ch 1, sc in each sc across to last 2 sts, sc2tog in last 2 sts, turn (15 sc).

Row 12: Ch 1, sc in each st across, turn (15 sc).

Row 13: Ch 1, sc in each sc across to last 2 sts, sc2tog in last 2 sts, turn (14 sc).

Rows 14–15: Ch 1, sc in each st across, turn (14 sc).

Row 16: Ch 1, sc2tog in first 2 sts, sc in each sc across, turn (13 sc).

Row 17: Ch 1, sc in each st across, turn (13 sc).

Row 18: Ch 1, sc2tog in first 2 sts, sc in each sc across, turn (12 sc).

Rows 19–20: Ch 1, sc in each st across, turn (12 sc).

Row 21: Ch 1, sc in each sc across to last 2 sts, sc2tog in last 2 sts, turn (11 sc).

Row 22: Ch 1, sc in each st across, turn (11 sc).

Rows 23–36: Rep Rows 21–22 (7 times) (4 sc at end of Row 36). Fasten off.

Motif C-1 (make 2)

With A, ch 27.

Row 1 (WS): Sc in 2nd ch from hook, sc in each ch across, turn (26 sc). Place a marker at beg of Row 1 for dec side.

Rows 2–3: Ch 1, sc in each st across, turn (26 sc).

Row 4: Ch 1, sc in each sc across to last 2 sts, sc2tog in last 2 sts, turn (25 sc).

Rows 5–7: Ch 1, sc in each st across, turn (25 sc).

Rows 8–27: Rep Rows 4–7 (5 times) (20 sc at end of Row 27).

Rows 28–30: Rep Rows 4–6 (19 sc at end of Row 30). Fasten off.

Motif C-2 (make 2)

Motif C-2 is the reverse shaping of Motif C-

With A, ch 27.

Row 1 (WS): Sc in 2nd ch from hook, sc in each ch across, turn (26 sc). Place a marker on this edge for dec side.

Rows 2–3: Ch 1, sc in each st across, turn (26 sc).

Row 4: Ch 1, sc2tog in first 2 sts, sc in each sc across, turn (25 sc).

Rows 5–7: Ch 1, sc in each st across, turn (25 sc).

Rows 8–27: Rep Rows 4–7 (5 times) (20 sc at end of Row 27).

Rows 28–30: Rep Rows 4–6 (19 sc at end of Row 30). Fasten off.

Motif D-1 (make 2)

With A, ch 20.

Row 1 (WS): Sc in 2nd ch from hook, sc in each ch across, turn (19 sc). Place a marker at beg of Row 1 for dec side.

Rows 2-4: Ch 1, sc in each st across, turn (19 sc).

Row 5: Ch 1, sc2tog in first 2 sts, sc in each sc across, turn (18 sc).

Rows 6–8: Ch 1, sc in each st across, turn (18 sc).

Rows 9–36: Rep Rows 5–8 (7 times) (11 sc at end of Row 36). Fasten off.

Motif D-2 (make 2)

Motif D-2 is the reverse shaping of Motif D-1

With A, ch 20.

Row 1 (WS): Sc in 2nd ch from hook, sc in each ch across, turn (19 sc). Place a marker on this edge for dec side

Rows 2–4: Ch 1, sc in each st across, turn (19 sc).

Row 5: Ch 1, sc in each sc across to last 2 sts, sc2tog in last 2 sts, turn (18 sc).

Rows 6–8: Ch 1, sc in each st across, turn (18 sc).

Rows 9–36: Rep Rows 5–8 (7 times) (11 sc at end of Row 36). Fasten off.

Motif E (make 2)

Bottom side pieces

With A, ch 12.

Row 1 (WS): Sc in 2nd ch from hook, sc in each ch across, turn (11 sc).

Rows 2–30: Ch 1, sc in each st across, turn (11 sc). Fasten off.

Motif F (make 2)

Top side pieces

With A, ch 12.

Row 1 (WS): Sc in 2nd ch from hook, sc in each ch across, turn (11 sc).

Rows 2–30: Ch 1, sc in each st across, turn (11 sc).

Rows 31–34: Ch 1, sc2tog in first 2 sts, sc in each sc across, sc2tog in last 2 sts, turn (3 sc at end of Row 34).

Row 35: Ch 1, sc3tog in next 3 sts (1 sc). Fasten off.

Finishing

Weave in ends. With right sides facing up, arrange motifs on a flat surface, following diagram for placement. With wrong sides facing, join motifs together, using 2 strands of B held together as one. Single crochet motifs together in columns. Crochet the columns together in same manner, making 2 identical pieces, a back and a front, with the side motifs attached. Then crochet the front and the back of the poncho together across the sides in the same way.

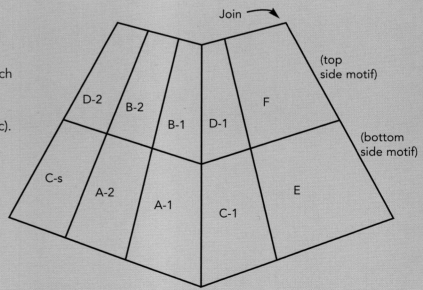

Front/Back (make 2) and join together across side

Neck Edging

With RS facing, join 2 strands of B on one side of neck edge.

Rnd 1: Ch 1, sc in each sc around, working sc2tog at each joining seam. Sl st in first sc to join.

Rnd 2: Ch 1, sc in each sc around, working sc2tog over each dec. Sl st in first sc to join. Fasten off.

Bottom Edging

With RS facing, join 2 strands of B on one side of bottom edge.

Rnd 1: Ch 1, sc in each sc around, working 3 sc at center front and back points. Sl st in first sc to join.

Rnd 2: Rep Rnd 1. Fasten off.

THIS PROJECT WAS CREATED WITH 10 skeins of Berroco *Suede* in Hopalong (#3714), 100% nylon, 1¾oz/50g = 120yd/110m

4 skeins of Berroco *Softy* in Snow Bunny (#2901), 52% DuPont Tactel Nylon, 48% Nylon, 1¾oz/50g = 104 yd/95m

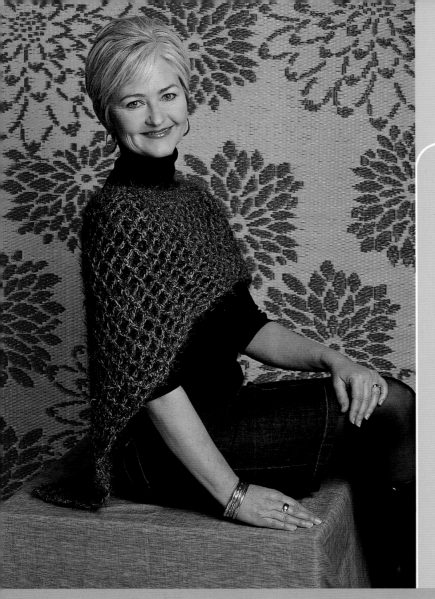

SKILL LEVEL: BEGINNER

FINISHED MEASUREMENTS
Women's sizes S (M, L)
Neck opening: 22 (26 ½, 31)"/56 (67, 79)cm circumference
Front length: 8 ½"/22cm from neck edge to bottom edge
Back length: 26 (28, 30)"/66 (71, 76)cm from neck edge to point

YOU WILL NEED
255 (255, 340)yd/233 (233,311)m of worsted weight yarn
Hook: size 6mm/J–10 or size needed to obtain gauge
Tapestry needle
Scissors
Stitch markers

STITCHES USED
Chain stitch (ch)
Double crochet (dc)
Half double crochet (hdc)
Single crochet (sc)
Slip stitch (sl st)

GAUGE
Take time to check your gauge.
9 sts = 4"/10cm; (sc, ch 4) 3 times and 6 rows in pattern = 4"/10cm

PATTERN NOTES
If you'd like to make larger or smaller sizes, begin with a chain that is divisible by 5 (5,10,15,20 etc.), then follow the pattern.
The beginning chain should fit over your head when it is stretched tightly. If you are unable to achieve desired neckline size, use a smaller or larger hook.

LOOKS GOOD FROM ANY ANGLE • *Designed by Freddie Schuh*

Crochet this poncho in a few evenings as designed or with fringe. Wear it with the tapered end to the side or the back. You'll find it looks great with everything you wear.

Pattern

Ch 50 (60, 70), and without twisting ch, join into a ring with sl st in first ch.

Neckline

Rnd 1: Ch 3, dc in each ch around. Sl st in 3rd ch of turning ch to join (50 [60, 70] sts).

Rnd 2: Ch 3, dc in each of next 3 dc, 2 dc in next dc, *dc in each of next 4 dc, 2 dc in next dc; rep from * around. Sl st in 3rd ch of turning ch to join (60 [72, 84] sts).

Rnd 3: Ch 1, sc in same place as joining, *ch 2, sk next dc, sc in next dc; rep from * around, ending with ch 1, sc in first sc to join (counts as last ch-2 sp) (30 [36, 42] ch-2 sps).

Rnd 4: Ch 1, sc in sp just made, ch 3, (sc, ch 3) in each loop around, ending with ch 1, hdc in first sc to join (counts as last ch-3 loop) (30 [36, 42] ch-3 loops).

Rnds 5–7: Ch 1, sc in sp just made ch 4, (sc, ch 4) in each loop around, ending with ch 1, dc in first sc to join (counts as last ch-4 loop) (30 [36, 42] ch-4 loops).

Rnd 8 (inc rnd): Counting loop just formed as 1st loop of last rnd, place a marker in 15th (18th, 21st) loop (this should be the number of loops on Rnd 7 divided by 2), ch 1, sc in loop just made, ch 4, (sc, ch 4) in each loop around to next marker, (sc, ch 4, sc) in marked loop, ch 4, (sc, ch 4) in each loop around to last loop, (sc, ch 4, sc) in last loop, ch 1, dc in first sc to join (32 [38, 44] ch-4 loops).

Rnds 9–11: Rep Rnd 5 (32 [38, 44] ch-4 loops).

Rnd 12 (inc rnd): Counting loop just formed as 1st loop of last rnd, place a marker in 16th (19th, 22st) loop (this should be the number of loops on Rnd 11 divided by 2), ch 1, sc in loop just made, ch 4, (sc, ch 4) in each loop around to next marker, (sc, ch 4, sc) in marked loop, ch 4, (sc, ch 4) in each loop around to last loop, (sc, ch 4, sc) in last loop, ch 1, dc in first sc to join (34 [40, 46] ch-4 loops).

Rnds 13–15: Rep Rnd 5.

Note: Continue to rep Rnd 5 until front measures desired length.

Tapered Bottom

Work now progresses in rows.

Row 16: Ch 4, turn, sc in next loop, ch 4, sc next loop, place a marker in this loop, ch 4, (sc, ch 4) in each loop across to last 4 loops, ch 1, dc in next loop, turn, leaving rem 3 loops unworked (30 [36, 42] loops).

Row 17: Ch 4, turn, sc in next loop, ch 4, sc next loop, place a marker in this loop, ch 4, (sc, ch 4) in each loop across to marked loop, ch 1, dc in marked loop, turn, leaving rem loops unworked (28 [34, 40] loops).

Rep Row 17 until only one loop rem. Fasten off. Weave in ends.

THIS PROJECT WAS CREATED WITH 3 (3, 4) balls of Euro Yarns, *On Line, Linie Spot* 73 (#0007), 1¾oz/50g, 85yd/78m

A poncho in the subtle color modulations of rusting metal makes a great fashion statement. Indulge your affinity for browns in all shades, textures, and fibers when you go shopping for yarns.

FREE-FORM RUST PONCHO • *Designed by Willena Nanton*

SKILL LEVEL: EASY

FINISHED MEASUREMENTS
One size fits most

YOU WILL NEED
Approx 1650yd/1485m of a variety of worsted and bulky weight yarns*
Rnds 8-9 of Shoulder and Neck Shaping call for a fake fur yarn.
Hook: 4.25mm/G-6 or size needed to obtain gauge
Stitch marker
Yarn Needle

*The designer used 18 different skeins of yarn in a variety of materials: mohair, wool, cotton, and manmade fibers. Use as many or as few colors and materials as desired. Work as many rounds of each color as desired or refer to specific yarns used at the end of pattern.

STITCHES USED
Chain stitch (ch)
Single crochet (sc)
Slip stitch (sl st)

SPECIAL STITCH TECHNIQUE
Single crochet decrease (sc2tog): (Insert hook in next st, yo, draw yarn through st) twice, yo, draw yarn through 3 loops on hook.

GAUGE
Take time to check your gauge.
15 sts and 18 rows sc = 4"/10cm.
Gauge will vary depending on yarn used.

Body

Starting at hip, with A, ch 191.

Row 1 (WS): Sc in 2nd ch from hook, sc in each ch across, turn (190 sc).

Row 2: Ch 1, sc in back lp of each sc across, turn (190 sc). Fasten off A.

Row 3: With WS facing, join B in first sc, ch 1, working in both loops of sts, sc in each sc across, turn (190 sc).

Row 4: Ch 1, sc in first sc, *sc in each of the next 3 sc, 2 sc in next sc; rep from * across to the last sc, sc in last sc, turn (237 sc).

Rows 5–14: Work even on 237 sc in the following color sequence: 2 rows B; 1 row C; 2 rows A; 1 row D; 2 rows A; 2 rows F. Do not turn at end of last row.

Note: The remaining rows will be worked in a spiral. Mark beg of each rnd. Move marker up as work progresses. To change color, sl st in next sc at end of last

rnd, join next color with sl st in same st, ch 1 to beginn next row.

Rnds 15–24: Sc in each sc around, working in the following color sequence: 5 rnds F; 5 rnds A.

Rnds 25–26: With A, sc in back lp of each sc around. Sl st in next sc to join. Fasten off A, join G.

Rnds 27–58: Sc in each sc around, working in the following color sequence: 4 rnds G; 1 rnd A; 6 rnds H, 2 rnds A; 3 rnds I; 1 rnd J; 1 rnd A; 5 rnds K; 2 rnds A; 1 rnd E; 2 rnds B; 2 rnds L; 1 rnd J; 1 rnd M; 1 rnd A.

Assembly

With WS facing, use yarn needle and matching color yarn to sew the back seam from Row 14 to Row 1.

Shaping Shoulders and Neck

Rnd 1: Working on the opposite side of the foundation ch, join A in the back seam, ch 1, sc in each st around, do not join, work in a spiral as before (190 sc).

Rnd 2: *Sc in each of the next 8 sc, sc2tog in next 2 sc; rep from * around (171 sts). Fasten off A, join B.

Rnd 3: With B, sc in each sc around (171 sc).

Rnd 4: *Sc in each of the next 5 sc, sc2tog in next 2 sc; rep from * around to the last 3 sc, sc in each of next 3 sc (147 sts).

Rnds 5–7: Rep Rnd 3 in the following color sequence: 1 more rnd B; 2 rnds C. At end of Rnd 7, turn. Fasten off C, join N.

Rnds 8–9: With WS facing, with N (a fake fur yarn), rep Rnd 3. At end of Rnd 9, turn. Fasten off N, join B.

Rnd 10: With RS facing, with B, rep Rnd 3.

Rnd 11: *Sc in each of the next 4 sc, sc2tog in next 2 sc; rep from * around to the last 3 sc, sc in each of next 2 sc (123 sts).

Rnd 12: *Sc in each of the next 3 sc, sc2tog in next 2 sc; rep from * around to the last 3 sc, sc in each of next 2 sc (99 sts).

Rnds 13–28: Rep Rnd 3 in the following color sequence: 2 rnds D; 2 rnds B; 3 rnds L; 6 rnds E; 2 rnds L. Fasten off. Weave in ends.

First Trim

Trim is worked across front side of poncho only. With seam at center back, flatten poncho and locate st of side fold to begin trim.

Row 1: With RS of Poncho facing, and bottom edge of poncho on top, working in remaining front lps of sts in Rnd 24 of body, join A in st on side fold to work across front, sc in rem loop of each of the next 119 sc, turn (119 sc).

Row 2: Sc in 1st sc, sc in each sc across. Fasten off.

Second Trim

Row 1: With RS of Poncho facing, and bottom edge of poncho on top, working in rem front lps of sts in Rnd 25 of Body, join A in st on side fold above 1st st on First Trim, sc in rem loop of each of the next 119 sc, turn (119 sc).

Row 2: Working through double thickness, in front lps of sts in Row 1 of Second Trim and front loops of sts in Row 2 of first trim, sc in each st across. Fasten off.

THIS PROJECT WAS CREATED WITH

A: 2 skeins of Lion Brand *Glitterspun* in Bronze (#135), 60% acrylic, 27% Cupro, 13% polyester, 1¾oz/50g = 115yd/105m

B: 4 skeins of Jo Sharp's *Soho Summer* in Java (#226), 100% Cotton, 1¾oz/50g = 109yd/100m

C: 1 skein of Katia FKI *Opera* in bronze (#56), 100% Nylon, 1¾oz/50g = 93yd/84m

D: 1 skein of Austermann's *Bueno* in brown with white (#09), 41% Wool/41% Acrylic/18% Nylon, 1¾oz/50g = 50yd/45m

E: 1 skein of Sirdar *Donegal Tweed* DK in Chocolate (#171),45% wool/30% polyester/25% acrylic, 1¾oz/50g = 133yd/121m

F: 1 skein of Spectrum *Batik* in variegated brown (#2), 98% Acrylic/2% Polyester, 2oz/57g

G: 1 skein of Red Heart *Classic*, 100% acrylic, 3 ½ oz/85g = 190yd/171m

H: 2 skeins of Schachenmayr's *La Nova* ribbon yarn in Cayenne (#87), 50% cotton/50% viscose, 2oz/57g = 99yd/90m

I: 1 skein of Plymouth Encore's *Worsted*, 75% acrylic/25% wool, 3 1/2 oz/100g = 200yd/180m

J: 1 skein of Lily's *Sugar n' Cream* Ombre in brown,, 100% cotton, 2oz/57g = 95yd/86m

K: 1 skein of -5 oz Lion Brand *Homespun* in Ranch (#326), 98% acrylic/2% polyester, 6oz/170g = 185yd/167m

L: 1 skein of Rowan *Lurex Shimmer* in bronze (#335), 80% viscose/20% polyester, 1oz/28g = 109yd/100m

M: 1 skein of *Flutter* (#009), 100% polyester, 20g =74yd/67m

N: 1 skein of Lion Brand *Fun Fur* in Copper (#134), 13/4oz/50g = 64yd/58m

Can you imagine wrapping yourself up in the warm glow of the sun setting in the west? If the answer is yes, then this heavenly soft poncho is a dream come true.

SUNSET PONCHO • *Designed by Donna May*

SKILL LEVEL: EASY

FINISHED MEASUREMENTS
One size fits most
Rectangles: 21 x 37"/53 x 94cm
Length: 30"/76cm from neck edge to center front point without collar/scarf

YOU WILL NEED
Approx 1064yd/973m bulky weight yarn
Hooks: 9mm/M–13 or size needed to obtain gauge
6.5mm/K–10 ½ for slip stitching seams (optional)
Stitch markers (optional)
Yarn needle
6"/15cm piece of cardboard
6 yd/6m of scrap yarn in contrasting color

STITCHES USED
Chain stitch (ch)
Half double crochet (hdc)
Single crochet (sc)
Slip stitch (sl st)

GAUGE
Take time to check your gauge.
9 sts and 7 rows hdc worked in back loop only = 4"/10cm

PATTERN NOTES
When starting a new ball of yarn, weave in ends before continuing.

Use a stitch marker or tie a piece of contrasting color yarn around a stitch on the first row of each piece to mark the right side. This will be very helpful when assembling the pieces.

For petites (5' 3"/160cm and under), or if a shorter poncho is desired, make the two rectangles 18 x 34"/46 x 86cm. In this case, total yarn requirement is approximately 896yd/806m.

Rectangle (make 2)
With M–13 hook, ch 49.

Row 1 (RS): Hdc in back loop of 3rd ch from hook, hdc in back loop of each ch across, turn (47 sts).

Rows 2–65: Ch 2, hdc in back loop of first hdc, hdc in back loop of each st across, turn (47 sts). Fasten off. Weave in ends.

Collar/Scarf
With M–13 hook, ch 24.

Row 1 (RS): Hdc in both loops of 3rd ch from hook, hdc in both loops of each ch across, turn (22 sts).

Rows 2–104: Ch 2, hdc in back loop of first hdc, hdc in back loop of each st across, turn (22 sts).

Row 105: Ch 2, hdc in both loops of first hdc, hdc in both loops of each st across, turn (22 sts). Fasten off. Weave in ends.

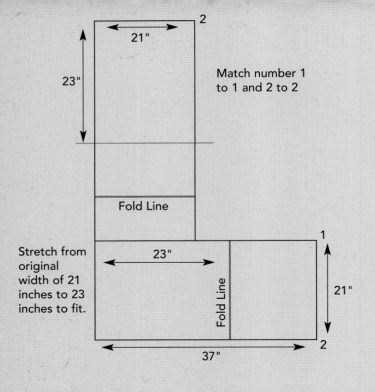

2

21"

23"

Match number 1
to 1 and 2 to 2

Fold Line

Stretch from
original
width of 21
inches to 23
inches to fit.

23"

Fold Line

1

21"

2

37"

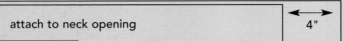

attach to neck opening

4"

Assembly

Using a stitch marker or a piece of contrasting color yarn, place a marker 23"/58cm from last row on left long edge of first rectangle (see figure ooo). With RS facing, center 1 short side of 2nd rectangle along the 23"/58cm section of first rectangle and evenly stretch the 2nd rectangle to 23"/58cm. Using contrasting yarn and long running stitches, baste 1"/25mm from edges along the 23"/58cm length. (If desired, slip stitch the seam using a size K–10 ½ crochet hook to make it easier to work in the stitches.) Remove basting stitches.

In the same manner, join short end of first Rectangle to side edge of 2nd Rectangle.

With contrasting yarn, baste long running stitches 1"/25mm below neck edge. Gently and evenly gather neck opening until its circumference measures 22"/56cm, Tie off basting yarn.

Lay Collar/Scarf piece lengthwise with right side down. Fold by bringing the left edge to within 4"/10cm of the right edge (wrong side will be on inside). With poncho body right side out and front of poncho facing you, hold right side of poncho neck opening in your left hand. Slide your left hand and poncho neck opening inside the folded collar/scarf and bring up the poncho neck opening so the corner meets the fold and the top edge of the collar/scarf. The right side of the poncho and the wrong side of the collar/scarf are facing each other.

With contrasting yarn, baste the collar/scarf to the neck opening using long running stitches 1"/25mm below edges. The scarf segments begin above the left shoulder, at the neck opening. This is where the basting stitches end. Tie off basting yarn.

Finishing

Slip stitch collar to poncho using a size K–10 ½ crochet hook, if desired. Fasten off. Weave in ends. Fold collar down.

Fringe

Use a 6"/15cm piece of cardboard to make 5"/13cm fringe, cut three 12"/30cm lengths of yarn for each fringe. Attach fringe approximately every ½"/13mm around lower edge of poncho and across each end of scarf. Trim fringe even.

THIS PROJECT WAS CREATED WITH 19 balls of South West Trading Company's *Diva* in Arizona Sunset, 78% acrylic/22% nylon, 1¾oz/50g = 56 yd/51m each

SKILL LEVEL: BEGINNER

FINISHED MEASUREMENTS
Women's sizes S (M, L)
Neck edge: 22 (26, 31)"/56 (66, 79)cm
Bottom edge: 54 (58, 63)"/137
(147, 160)cm
Length: 17"/43cm plus fringe
Child's
Neck edge: 17"/43cm
Bottom edge: 38"/96cm
Length: 10"/25cm plus fringe

YOU WILL NEED
Adult sizes: Approx 300 (352,400)yd/274
(322, 366)cm worsted weight yarn
Chilld's size: Approx 300yd/274cm
worsted weight yarn.
Hook: size 6mm (J-10 U.S.) or size
needed to obtain gauge
Tapestry needle
Stitch marker

STITCHES USED
Chain stitch (ch)
Double crochet (dc)
Half double crochet (hdc)
Single crochet (sc)
Slip stitch (sl st)

GAUGE
Take time to check your gauge
Gauge: 10 sts = 4"/10cm

PERFECT PAIR OF PONCHOS • *Designed by Freddie Schuh*

Go ahead: Make one for yourself and for your daughter, granddaughter, niece, or best friend.

To make this poncho in a larger size, add 200yd/183m for every 10"/25cm of length before fringe.

For a larger or smaller neck opening, chain any multiple of 6 stitches to fit over the head when stretched tightly. If you're unable to achieve desired size neckline, use a larger hook.

Directions are written for a woman's size S (M,L) in any worsted weight yarn. If you'd like to make another size, or use a different weight of yarn, just begin with a chain which is divisible by 6 (6,12,18, 24 etc), then follow directions given below. Any yarn that fringes well will produce the look illustrated in the photo.

Adult Version

Ch 54 (66, 78), without twisting ch, close into a ring with 1 sl st in first ch.

Rnd 1: Ch 3, dc in each of next 4 ch, 2 dc in next ch, *dc in each of next 5 ch, 2 dc in next ch; rep from * around. Sl st to 3rd ch of turning ch to join (63 [77, 91] dc).

Rnd 2: Ch 3, dc in each of next 5 ch, 2 dc in next ch, *dc in each of next 72 ch, 2 dc in next ch; rep from * around. Sl st to 3rd ch of turning ch to join (72 [88, 104] dc).

Body

Rnd 3: Ch 1, sc in first st, *ch 3, sk next dc, sc in next dc; rep from * around to last st, sk next sc, ch 1, hdc in first sc to join (last loop made) (36 [44, 52] loops)

Rnd 4: Ch 1, sc in loop just made, *ch 4, sc in next loop; rep from * around to last loop, ch 1, dc in first sc to join (last loop made) (36 [44, 52] loops).

Rnds 5–6: Rep Rnd 4, placing a stitch marker on the 18th (22nd, 26th) loop in Rnd 6.

Increase Round

Rnd 7: Ch 1, sc in loop just made, *ch 4, sc in next loop*; rep from * to * around to marker, (ch 4, sc in marked loop) twice, rep from * to * around to last loop, (ch 4, sc in last loop on round) twice, ch 1, dc in first sc to join round (last loop made) (38 [46, 54] loops).

Rnds 8–10: Rep Rnd 4, placing a stitch marker on the 19th (23rd, 27th) loop on Rnd 10.

Rnd 11: Rep Rnd 7 (40 [48, 56] loops).

Rnds 12–14: Rep Rnd 4, placing a stitch marker on the 20th (24th, 28th) loop in Rnd 14.

Rnd 15: Rep Rnd 7 (42 [50, 58] loops).

Rnds 16–18: Rep Rnd 4, placing a stitch marker on the 2first (25th, 29th) loop in Rnd 18.

Rnd 19: Rep Rnd 7 (44 [52, 60] loops).

Rnds 20–22: Rep Rnd 4, placing a stitch marker on the 22nd (26th, 30th) loop in Rnd 22.

Rnd 23: Rep Rnd 7 (46 [54, 62] loops).

Rnds 24–26: Rep Rnd 4. Fasten off. Weave in ends. Continue in this manner to add rows for a longer poncho or omit rows for a shorter version.

Child's Version

Directions are written so you can make any child-size poncho in any length.

Ch 42 and without twisting ch, close into a ring with 1 sl st in first ch.

Rnd 1: Ch 3, dc in each of next 4 ch, 2 dc in next ch, *dc in each of next 5 ch, 2 dc in next ch; rep from * around. Sl st to 3rd ch of turning ch to join (49 dc).

Work same as adult's through Rnd 15 or for desired length. Fasten off leaving an 8"/20cm tail. Weave in ends.

Finishing

Cut 69 (81, 93) 12"/30 cm strands of yarn (or enough strands to place 3 strands in every other loop around). Using 3 strands for each fringe, single knot one fringe in every other loop around last round of poncho as follows: Fold 3 strands in half. Insert hook in loop on bottom edge of poncho and put folded strands over hook, pulling through slightly. Pull yarn ends through fold. You may allow the strands to unravel naturally over time or encourage the strands to unravel by splitting them one at a time.

For a snappier and totally unique look, experiment with ribbon, ladder, or other novelty yarn in the same colorway as your poncho for fringe.

THESE PROJECTS WERE CREATED WITH 4 balls of Plymouth *Sunsette* #68, 60% rayon/40% acrylic, 1 ¾oz/50g = 88yd/80m

2 balls of Plymouth *Sunsette* #202, 60% rayon/40% acrylic, 1 ¾oz/50g = 88yd/80m

A designer's stash of lightweight wool yarn inspired this poncho that drapes beautifully and seems to float on the body.

yarn through st, yo, draw yarn through 2 loops on hook) 4 times, yo, draw yarn through all loops on hook.

6-dc cluster: (Yo, insert hook in next st, yo, draw yarn through st, yo, draw yarn through 2 loops on hook) 6 times, yo, draw yarn through all loops on hook.

PATTERN NOTES
Work in the following color sequence: *1 row D; 3 rows A; 1 row E; 3 rows B; 1 row D; 3 rows C; 1 row E; 3 rows A; 1 row D; 3 rows B; 1 row E; 3 rows C; rep from * once, 1 row D.

LOPI PONCHO • *Design by Dora Ohrenstein*

SKILL LEVEL: EASY

FINISHED MEASUREMENTS
Women's sizes S/M (L)
Neck opening: 24 (30)"/61 (76)cm in circumference
Width: 38 (41)"/97 (104)cm across bottom edge
Length: 23"/58cm from neck edge to bottom edge

YOU WILL NEED
Approx 327yd/294m each of 3 colors worsted weight wool yarn: olive (A), khaki (B), lime (C)
Approx 218yd/196m each of 2 colors worsted weight wool yarn: blue (D), red (E).
Hook: sizes 5.5mm/I-9 and 5mm/H-8 or size needed to obtain gauge

GAUGE
Take time to check your gauge.

With I-9 hook, 13 sts and 9 rows hdc in pattern = 4"/10cm; with H-8 hook, 14 sts = 4"/10cm

STITCHES USED
Chain stitch (ch)
Half double crochet (hdc)
Slip stitch (sl st)

SPECIAL STITCH TECHNIQUES
Front post double crochet (fpdc): Yo, insert hook from front to back to front again, around the post of designated st 2 rows below, yo, draw yarn through st and up to level of current row, (yo, draw yarn through 2 loops on hook) twice.
Half double crochet decrease (hdc2tog): (Yo, insert hook in next st and draw up a loop) twice, yo, draw through all loops on hook.
4-dc cluster: (Yo, insert hook in next st, yo, draw

Front/Back (make 2)

Starting at bottom edge, with D, ch 110 (120)

Row 1: Hdc in 3rd ch from hook hdc in each ch across, turn (109 [119] sts). Fasten off D, join A.

Row 2: Ch 2, hdc in each st across, turn (109 [119] sts).

Row 3: Ch 2, hdc in each of next 8 sts, *fpdc around the post of next corresponding st 2 rows below, skip hdc behind fpdc just made, hdc in each of next 9 sts* rep from * across, turn (109 [119] sts).

Row 4: Ch 2, hdc in each st across, turn (109 [119] sts). Fasten off A, join E.

Row 5: With E, rep Row 3.

Rep Rows 3–5 for pattern throughout body

Rows 6–17: Maintaining color sequence as established, rep Rows 2–5 (3 times).

Maintaining color as established throughout, decrease at each end of 3 rows of wide stripes, work even in each 1-row stripe through Row 33 as follows:

Row 18: Ch 2, hdc2tog in next 2 sts (dec made), hdc in each st across to turning ch, turn leaving remaining st unworked (dec made) (107 [117] sts).

Row 19: Ch 2, hdc2tog in next 2 sts (dec made), maintaining established pattern of Row 3 across to turning ch, turn leaving remaining st unworked (dec made) (105 [115] sts).

Row 20: Rep Row 18 (103 [113] sts)

Row 21: Work even in established pattern of Row 3 (103 [113] sts).

Rows 22–24: Work in established pattern, dec 1 st at each end of each row as established (97 [107] sts at end of Row 24).

Row 25: Work even in established pattern across, turn (97 [107] sts).

Row 26: Rep Row 18 (95 [105] sts).

Row 27: Ch 2, skip first 2 hdc, (dec made) *fpdc around the post of next corresponding st 2 rows below, skip hdc behind fpdc just made, hdc in each

of next 9 sts* rep from * across to last 2 sts, hdc in next st, turn leaving remaining st unworked (dec made) (93 [103] sts).

Row 28: Rep Row 18 (91 [101] sts).

Row 29: Work even in established pattern (91 [101] sts).

Rows 30–32: Maintaining established pattern and color sequence, dec 1 st at each end of every row (85 [95] sts).

Row 33: Work even in established pattern (85 [95] sts).

Rows 34–49: Maintaining established pattern and color sequence, dec 1 st at each end of every row (53 [63] sts at end or Row 49). Fasten off. Weave in ends.

Assembly

With wrong sides facing, use a yarn needle and matching color yarn to sew side seams from Row 18 (first decrease row) to top edge, leaving the first 17 rows unjoined for slits.

Neck Edging

Rnd 1: With RS of Poncho facing, using H-8 hook, join E in 3 sts to the left of 1 side seam, ch 2, *4-dc cluster across next 4 sts, hdc in each st across to within 2 sts of next side seam; rep from * once, complete last st with D. Sl st in 2nd ch of turning ch to join.

Rnd 2: With D, ch 2, hdc in each st around, working 6-dc cluster centered over each cluster at sides, complete last st with E. Sl st in 2nd ch of turning ch to join.

Rnds 3-4: With E, rep Rnd 1, at end of Rnd 4, complete last st with D.

Rnd 5: With D, sl st in each st around. Fasten off.

Slit Edging

Row 1: With right side of poncho facing, use I-9 hook to join D in corner stitch on bottom edge of one slit, do not ch 2, starting in base of first st in Row 2, work 23 hdc evenly spaced across to top of slit, work 23 hdc evenly spaced across to base of Row 2, sl st in corner on lower edge of Row 1. Fasten off. Rep Row 1 across other slit.

Bottom Edging

Rnd 1: With right side of poncho facing, using I-9 hook, join E in corner st on one bottom edge, ch 2, hdc evenly around entire bottom edge, working 3 hdc in each corner st and hdc2tog at top of each slit. Sl st in 2nd ch of turning ch to join. Fasten off E, join D.

Rnd 2: With D, rep Rnd 2.

THIS PROJECT WAS CREATED WITH 3 skeins each of Reynolds *Lite-Lopi* in Celery Heather (#421), Gold Heather (#426), and Leaf (#441), 1¾oz/50g =109yd/100m

2 skeins each of Reynolds *Lite-Lopi* in Ocean (#419), and Maroon (#414), 1 3/4oz/50g =109yd/100m

Work rectangles in the round rather than back and forth. This impressive-looking poncho is a great way to use a wide variety of yarns to create a unique look.

neck border and fringe. To add on new color, make slipknot, insert hook in desired stitch, place slipknot on hook and draw through work, begin row. Join a different color for each row, creating contrast in color and texture throughout. Leave an 8"/20cm tail on left-hand side of first half and on same side when working 2nd side.

Work lighter weight yarns with 2 strands held together tocreate a more interesting texture and color.

MODULAR CROCHET PONCHO • *Designed by Dee Stanzio*

SKILL LEVEL: EASY

FINISHED MEASUREMENTS
On size fits most
Each rectangle: 14 x 40"/36 x102cm
Neck opening: 28"/71cm in circumference
Length: 28"/71cm from V on neck edge to center front point

YOU WILL NEED
Approx 1500yd/1350m worsted, chunky, sport, and bulky weight yarns in different textures including mohairs, bouclés, slubs, and ribbon, metallics, smooth, eyelash, and novelty yarns. Use yarns of manmade and natural fibers as desired.
Hook: size 7mm/K–10½ or size needed to obtain gauge
Yarn needle
Stitch markers (8 or more)

STITCHES USED
Chain stitch (ch)
Double crochet (dc)
Half double crochet (hdc)

Single crochet (sc)
Slip stitch (sl st)

SPECIAL STITCH TECHNIQUES
Decrease 2 double crochet (dc3tog): (Yo, insert hook in next st and draw up a loop, yo and draw through 2 loops) 3 times, yo, draw through all loops on hook.
Decrease 2 half double crochet (hdc3tog): (Yo, insert hook in next st and draw up a loop) 3 times, yo, draw through all loops on hook.
Decrease 2 single crochet (sc3tog): (Insert hook in next st and draw up a loop) 3 times, yo, draw through all loops on hook.

GAUGE
Take time to check your gauge.
10 sts = 4"/10cm

PATTERN NOTES
This poncho was created with Judith Copeland's modular crochet technique. The rectangles are worked from the center out, then assembled with an added

Rectangle (make 2)

First Side

Leaving an 8"/20cm tail, with first color, ch 101.

Row 1 (RS): Sc in next 2nd ch from hook, sc in each ch across. Fasten off leaving 8"/20cm tail (100 sts).

Row 2: Leaving an 8"/20cm tail, join next color, ch 2 (does not count as a st), hdc in first st, hdc in each st across, turn (100 sc). Fasten off.

Row 3: Join next color, ch 3, skip first st, dc in each st across, turn (100 sts). Fasten off leaving an 8"/20cm tail.

Rows 4–15: Continue to join a new color at beginning of each row, leaving an 8"/20cm fringe length on left-hand side of Rectangle, work 1 more row dc; 3 rows hdc; 3 rows sc; 3 rows dc; 1 row hdc; 1 row sc. Fasten off. Mark last row as top edge of rectangle.

Second Side

Row 1: With RS of first side facing, working across opposite side of foundation ch, with fringe lengths on the right, leaving an 8"/20cm tail, join choice of color in first ch, ch 1, sc each ch across, turn (100 sc). Fasten off.

Rows 2–12: Continue to join a new color at beginning of each row, leaving an 8"/20cm fringe length on right-hand side of rectangle, work 2 rows dc; 3 rows hdc; 3 rows dc; 1 row hdc; 2 rows dc. Fasten off. Weave in ends on side opposite fringe.

Assembly

On top edge of first rectangle, place a marker in 40th stitch from fringed edge. Repeat on the second rectagle. Lay unfringed, short edge of second rectangle across the 40 stitch marked section. Pin rectangles together. With yarn needle and matching yarn, sew pieces together. Sew unfringed short end of first rectangle to first 40 stitches on top edge of second rectangle. Ensure areas marked top are facing neckline.

Neck Border

Rnd 1: With RS facing, join choice of color on neck edge, 3 sts before the junction that forms the V in the neckline, ch 3, dc in next st, dc3tog across next 3 sts, dc in next 58 sts, dc3tog across next 3 sts, dc in rem 56 sts. Sl st in 3rd ch of turning ch to join. Fasten off.

Rnd 2: With RS facing, join next color in 3rd st before the decrease at center V, ch 2, hdc in next st, hdc3tog across next 3 sts, hdc in each st across to 1 st before next dec, hdc3tog across next 3 sts, hdc in rem st around. Sl st in 2nd ch of turning ch to join. Fasten off.

Rnd 3: With RS facing, join next color in 3rd st before the decrease at center V, ch 3, dc in next st, dc3tog across next 3 sts, dc in each st across to 1 st before next dec, dc3tog across next 3 sts, dc in rem st around. Sl st in 3rd ch of turning ch to join. Fasten off.

Rnd 4: Rep Rnd 2

Rnd 5: With RS facing, join next color in 3rd st before the dec at center V, ch 1, sc in first 2 sts, sc3tog across next 3 sts, sc in each st across to 1 st before next dec, sc3tog across next 3 sts, sc in rem st around. Sl st in first sc to join. Fasten off.

Rnd 6: Rep Rnd 3.

Rnds 7–8: Rep Rnds 2-3.

Rnd 9: Rep Rnd 5. Fasten off.

Fringe

Cut leftover yarn into 16"/41cm lengths. Using 2 strands of yarn for each fringe, choosing colors randomly, place 1 fringe in each st around entire bottom edge of poncho, incorporating yarn tails into the fringe.

THIS PROJECT WAS CREATED WITH 1 skein of Filatura Di Crosa's *Zara* (#1499), 100% extra fine merino wool, 1¾oz/50g = 137yd/123m

1 skein of Di. Ve' *Fiamma Stampato* (#12798), 100% wool, 1¾oz/50g = 55yd/50m

1 skein of Berroco *Quest* (#9825), 100% nylon, 1¾oz/50g = 82yd/76m

1 skein Linie 73 *Spot* (#03), 48% polyamid/40% polyacryl/12% tactel, 1¾ozoz/50g = 83yd/75m

1 skein of Karabella's *Aurora* 8 in teal, 100% Merino wool, 1¾oz/50g = 98yd/88m

1 skein of *Flutter* (#47), 100% polyester, 20g =74yd/67m

1 skein of Skacel's *Tropicana* in blue variegated, 97% nylon/3% metal polyester, 25g = 55yd/50m

1 skein of *Fonty Velourine* (#569), 54% cotton/46% viscose, 1¾oz/50g = 119yd/107m

1 skein of The Great Adirondack Yarn Co.'s *Whisker Royal*, 100% polyester, 75yd/68m

1 skein of Berroco's *Lavish* in Cadaquez , 40% nylon/32% wool/13% acrylic, 55yd/50m

1 skein of Berroco's *Quest* in Criptonite (#9823), 100% nylon, 1¾oz/50g = 82yd/76m

1 skein *Gioco Filpucci* (#13), 100% polyamid, 1¾oz/50g = 149yd/134m

1 skein Trendsetter Yarns' Metal in teal, 100% polyester, 20g = 75yd/68m

1 skein of *Orlando* in teal, 100% polyester, 1¾ozoz/50g = 83yd/75m

1 skein of Knit One Crochet Too's *Tartelette* in Blueberry (#630), 50% cotton/40% tactel nylon/10% nylon, 1¾oz/50g = 75yd/68m

1 skein of Lana Gatto's *Crystal* (#4115), 63% viscose/20% nylon/17% polyester, 1¾oz/50g = 87yd/78m

SKILL LEVEL: EASY

FINISHED MEASUREMENTS
One size fits most
Neck edge: 84"/213cm circumference
Bottom edge: 84"/213cm circumference
Length: 18"/46cm from neck to bottom edge excluding fringe

YOU WILL NEED
Approx 556yd/508cm worsted weight yarn (A)
Approx 110yd/100m ribbon yarn (B)
Hook: size 8mm/L–11 or size needed to obtain gauge
23 gold-tone pony beads
Yarn needle

STITCHES USED
Chain stitch (ch)
Double crochet (dc)
Single crochet (sc)
Slip stitch (sl st)

SPECIAL STITCH TECHNIQUE
Extended single crochet (esc): Insert hook in next st yo, draw yarn through st, yo, draw through 1 loop on hook, yo, draw through 2 loops on hook.

GAUGE
Take time to check your gauge.
8 sts and 9 rows sc = 4"/10cm; 4 rows dc = 4"/10cm

FESTIVE PONCHO • *Designed by Freddie Schuh*

Could there be a more festive trim combination than silky ribbon yarn and beads? The fluid-moving trim comes to life when you move. Anyone in the mood for dancing?

Pattern

With A, ch 69 and, without twisting ch, close into a ring with 1 sl st in first ch.

Rnd 1: Ch 1, sc in each ch around. Sl st in first sc to join (69 sc).

Rnd 2: Ch 1, sc in each sc around. Sl st in first sc to join (69 sc).

Rnd 3: Ch 1, *sc in each of next 2 sc, 2 sc in next sc; rep from * around. Sl st in first sc to join (92 sc).

Rnd 4: Ch 1, sc in each sc around. Sl st in first sc join (92 sc).

Rnd 5: Ch 1, *sc in each of next 3 sc, 2 sc in next sc; rep from * around. Sl st in first sc to join (115 sc).

Rnds 6–8: Rep Row 4 (115 sc).

Rnd 9: Ch 1, sc in each of next 2 sc, *2 sc in next sc, sc in each of next 3 sc, 2 sc in next sc, sc in each of next 2 sc; rep from * around. Sl st in first sc join (148 sc).

Rnd 10: Rep Row 4 (147 sc).

Rnds 11-12: Ch 2, 1 esc in each st around. Sl st in first esc to join (148 esc).

Rnds 13-24: Ch 3, dc in each st around. Sl st in first dc to join (148 dc).

Rnds 25–26: Rep Rnd 11 (148 esc). Fasten off.

Neck fringe

Cut 69 strands of B, 11"/28cm long. Using one strand for each fringe, single knot one fringe around the post of each sc in Rnd 1 as follows: Fold strand in half. Insert hook from front to back to front again, around the post of sc, put folded strands over hook pulling through slightly. With folded strand remaining on hook, yo and pull yarn ends through fold. Using a small crochet hook, slide 1 bead to top of 1 fringe end, tie fringe end in an overhand knot close to bead to secure. Attach 1 bead to every 3rd fringe around neck edge. Trim fringe even.

Bottom fringe

Cut B into 37 strands 11"/28cm long, 111 pieces 14"/36cm long, and 74 pieces 18"/46cm long. Use two 14"/36cm and one 11"/28cm length for Fringe A. Use two 18"/46cm and one 14"/36cm length for Fringe B. Attach one fringe in every other st around bottom edge of poncho, alternating A and B fringe around.

THIS PROJECT WAS CREATED WITH 2 skeins of TLC *Amore* in Celery (#3625), 80% acrylic/20% nylon, 6oz/170g = 278yd/254m

1 ball of Lion Brand *Incredible* in Copper Penny (#520)
1 ball 100% nylon, 1¾oz/50g = 110yd/100m

This unusual garment—a poncho variation with sleeves—is flattering to all figure types. The front and back shaping creates an attractive funnel neckline.

SLEEVED PONCHO • *Designed by Jenny King*

SKILL LEVEL: EASY

FINISHED MEASUREMENTS
One size fits most
Length: 24"/61cm from neck edge to bottom edge at center front
Neck opening: 18"/46cm in circumference

YOU WILL NEED
Approx 1200yd/1080m DK or light worsted weight yarn

Hooks: size 3.5mm/E-4 or size needed to obtain gauge, and size 3.25mm/D-3 for cuffs
Yarn needle
Stitch markers

STITCHES USED
Chain stitch (ch)
Double crochet (dc)
Front post double crochet (fpdc)
Single crochet (sc)
Slip stitch (sl st)

GAUGE
Take time to check your gauge.
22 sts and 9 rows dc = 4"/10cm

PATTERN NOTES
All increases occur on the shoulder/side seams.

Pattern

Starting at neck edge, using E-4 hook, ch 100 and, without twisting ch, close into a ring with 1 sl st in first ch.

Rnd 1: Ch 4 (counts as dc, ch 1), skip next ch, *dc in next ch, ch 1, skip next ch; rep from * around. Sl st to 3rd ch of turning ch to join (50 ch-1 sps).

Rnd 2: Sl st in first ch-1 sp, ch 4, dc, ch 1 in same space (center back inc), (dc, ch 1) in each of next 25 dc, (dc, ch 1, dc, ch 1) in next ch-1 sp (center front inc), (dc, ch 1) in each of next 25 dc. Sl st to 3rd ch of turning ch to join (54 ch-1 sps). Place a stitch marker in each inc sp at center back and center front, move markers up as work progresses.

Rnd 3: Sl st in first ch-1 sp, ch 4 (counts as dc, ch 1), dc, ch 1 in same space (center back inc), (dc, ch 1) in each dc around to next marked sp, (dc, ch 1, dc, ch 1) in next marked sp (center front inc), (dc, ch 1) in each dc around. Sl st to 3rd ch of turning ch to join (58 ch-1 sps).

Rnds 4–6: Rep Rnd 3 (70 ch-1 spaces at end of Row 6).

Shoulder Shaping

Rnd 7: Ch 4 (counts as dc, ch 1), (dc, ch 1) in each of next 17 dc, (dc, ch 1, dc, ch 1) in next ch-1 sp (shoulder shaping), (dc, ch 1) in each of next 34 dc, (dc, ch 1, dc, ch 1) in next ch-1 sp (shoulder shaping), (dc, ch 1) in each of next 16 dc. Sl st to 3rd ch of turning ch to join (74 ch-1 sps). Place a marker in each inc sp at shoulders, move markers up as work progresses.

Rnd 8: Ch 4 (counts as dc, ch 1), (dc, ch 1) in each dc around to next marked sp, (dc, ch 1, dc, ch 1) in next marked ch-1 sp (shoulder shaping), (dc, ch 1) in each dc around to next marked sp, (dc, ch 1, dc, ch 1) in next marked ch-1 sp (shoulder shaping), (dc, ch 1) in each dc around. Sl st to 3rd ch of turning ch to join (78 ch-1 sps).

Rnds 9–56: Rep Rnd 8 (270 ch-1 sps at end of Rnd 56).

Rnd 57: Ch 4 (counts as dc, ch 1), (dc, ch 1) in each dc around. Sl st to 3rd ch of turning ch to join (270 ch-1 sps). Fasten off.

Assembly

Place a marker in 10th dc on each side of each inc in Row 56. With RS facing, flatten poncho so that folds lie on shoulder inc lines and markers are aligned. Leaving last 10 sps free on each side of bottom edge for cuff opening, sew a 4½"/11cm seam from marked st toward center of poncho.

Cuffs

Rnd 1: With RS of poncho facing, using F-5 hook, join yarn in first ch-1 sp to the left of sleeve seam on bottom edge of cuff opening, ch 1, *sc in ch-1 sp, fpdc around the post of next dc; rep from * around. Sl st in first sc to join.

Rnd 2: Ch 1, *sc in back loop only of sc, fpdc around the post of next dc; rep from * around. Sl st in first sc to join.

Rep Rnd 2 until cuff measures 4"/10cm from beg. Fasten off. Weave in ends.

Bottom Edging

With RS of Poncho facing, using E-4 hook, attach yarn on one sleeve seam on bottom edge, ch 1, working from right to left, reverse sc in each ch-1 sp around. Sl st in first reverse sc to join.

Neck Edging

With RS of Poncho facing, using E-4 hook, join yarn in any ch-1 sp on neck edge, ch 1, working from right to left, reverse sc in each ch-1 sp around. Sl st in first reverse sc to join.

THIS PROJECT WAS CREATED WITH 14oz/400gms = 1200yd/1080 DK weight wool yarn

Who says, it's not easy being green? Not the designer of this poncho. Essentially, you make a long scarf, then join it to make a seam. Anyone can make a scarf, so you can make a poncho!

SUPER EASY RIBBON PONCHO • *Designed by Jenny King*

SKILL LEVEL: EASY

FINISHED MEASUREMENTS
One size fits most

YOU WILL NEED
Approx 480yd/432m
worsted weight
ribbon yarn
Hook: size 16mm/Q or
size needed to obtain
gauge

STITCHES USED
Chain stitch (ch)
Single crochet (sc)
Slip stitch (sl st)

GAUGE
*Take time to check
your gauge.*
8 sts and 8 rows sc
worked in front loop only
= 4"/10cm

PATTERN NOTES
All stitches are worked in
the front loop only.
This is a long scarf which
when complete has the
first 25 stitches and last 25
stitches of foundation
chain sewn together as a
shoulder seam.

Pattern

Leaving a 31½"/80cm tail, ch 86.

Row 1: Sc in 2nd ch from hook, sc in each ch across, turn (85 sc).

Row 2: Ch 1, sc in front loop only of each sc across, turn (85 sc).

Rep Row 2 for 39 rows or until yarn runs out, completing last row. Fasten off.

Assembly

Fold poncho in half. Matching first and last 25 stitches of foundation chain, sew shoulder seam using a yarn needle and ribbon yarn.

THIS PROJECT WAS CREATED WITH 6 balls of Crystal Palace *Deco Ribbon* (#302), 70% acrylic/30% nylon, 1¾oz/50g = 80yd/72m

Bold stripes of color magically become subtle when you create an airy mesh with treble stitches. Personalize the poncho with your favorite colors, or opt for a single shade—either way you'll turn heads.

TRICOLOR MESH PONCHO • *Designed by Kalpna Kapoor*

SKILL LEVEL: BEGINNER

FINISHED MEASUREMENTS
One size fits most
24"/61cm wide x
21½"/55cm long plus fringe

YOU WILL NEED
360yd/914m worsted
weight suede-look yarn in
each of 3 colors:
Olive (A), Tan (B), and
Blue (C)
Hook: size 5mm/H-8 or size
to obtain gauge

STITCHES USED
Chain stitch (ch)
Double crochet (dc)
Single crochet (sc)
Slip stitch (sl st)
Treble crochet (tr)

GAUGE
*Take time to check
your gauge.*
20 sts and 5 rows tr =
4"/10cm

Starting at bottom edge, with A, ch 247.

Row 1: Tr in 11th ch from hook, *ch 3, skip next 3 ch, tr in next ch; rep from * across, turn (60 ch-3 sps).

Row 2: Ch 7 (counts as tr, ch 3), (ch 3, tr) in each tr across to last loop, skip next 3 ch, tr in next ch, turn (60 ch-3 sps).

Rows 3–9: Rep Row 2. Fasten off A, join B.

Rows 10–18: With B, rep Row 2. Fasten off B, join C.

Rows 19–27: With C, rep Row 2. Fasten off C.

Finishing

Fold poncho in half crosswise. Match stitches across the top edge. Use a yarn needle and yarn C, sew the shoulder seam across first 18 spaces from outer edge toward folded edge, leaving center 24 spaces unsewn for the neck opening.

Neck Edging

With right side of poncho facing, join one strand each of A and B held together as one in shoulder seam on neck edge, chain 1, single crochet evenly around neck opening. Slip stitch in the first single crochet to join.

Fringe

Cut 12"/30cm lengths of yarn. Using 2 strands of each color together for each fringe, single knot one fringe in each loop across bottom edge and side edge of poncho as follows: fold 3 strands in half. Insert hook in loop on edge of poncho and put folded strands over hook pulling through slightly. With folded strands remaining on hook, yarn over and pull yarn ends through fold. Trim fringe even.

THIS PROJECT WAS CREATED WITH 3 balls each of Berroco Suede in (A) Wrangler (#3704), (B) Hopalong Cassidy (#3715) and (C) Tonto (3714), 100% nylon, 1 ¾oz/50g = 120 yd/110m

This autumn potpourri is a fun opportunity to mix and match yarns you already have in your stash. Special features such as the slits for your arms, a scarf that grows out of the collar, and the charming little boxes of color make this a standout.

through st, yo, draw yarn through 2 loops on hook) 3 times, yo, draw yarn through all loops on hook.
Half double crochet decrease (hdc2tog): (Yo, insert hook in next st, yo, draw yarn through st) twice, yo, draw yarn through all loops on hook.

GAUGE
Take time to check your gauge
Using K–10 ½ hook and 1 strand each of A an C held together as one, 10 sts = 4"/10cm; 2 rows dc + 4 rows hdc = 3.5"/8.9 cm.

AUTUMN POTPOURRI • *Design by Dora Ohrenstein*

SKILL LEVEL: INTERMEDIATE

FINISHED MEASUREMENTS
Women's sizes S (M, L)
Neck width (across collar):
18 (18, 21)"/46 (46, 53)cm
Bottom width (before border): 60 (64, 67)"/152 (163,170)cm across
Length (collar to edge):
28"/71cm

YOU WILL NEED
985yd/900m worsted weight yarn in tan (A)
200yd/183m worsted weight yarn in charcoal (B)
1185yd/1084m mohair yarn in tan (C)
300yd/274m thick/thin bulky weight variegated yarn (D)
70yd/64m sport weight yarn for collar/scarf (E)
82yd/75m fake fur yarn for border (F)
Hooks: 6.5mm/K–10 ½ and 6.00mm/J–10 or sizes needed to obtain gauge

STITCHES USED
Chain stitch (ch)
Double crochet (dc)
Half double crochet (hdc)

SPECIAL STITCH TECHNIQUES
Double crochet decrease (dc2tog): (Yo, insert hook in next st, yo, draw yarn through st, yo, draw yarn through 2 loops on hook) twice, yo, draw yarn through all loops on hook.
Decrease 2 double crochet (dc3tog): (Yo, insert hook in next st, yo, draw yarn

PATTERN NOTES
Crochet small swatches to dtermine the best yarn/color combinations.

This is one-piece design with no seams, starts at the bottom. The shape gradually narrows to the shoulder, decreasing in every other row on both sides.

The arm slits are created by working three separate pieces (left, right, and back) for 10 rows. Little boxes in contrasting color are inserted at regular intervals in double crochet rows. Random strips are added on even numbered rows of half double crochet.

Little Boxes: These use a contrasting worsted weight (C) (here charcoal) and the mohair (B) that matches the worsted weight (A) of the body; carry color A on wrong side. When beginning and finishing the box, do not work over the tails of the contrasting worsted, rather, give them a tug when you work the next row of stitches to keep them tight. Later these tails will be woven in. Work blocks as indicated in Rows 3 and 4. In later rows, position blocks directly over blocks in specified row (3 or 4). Exact position of blocks is not critical.

Random Strips: No stitch counts are given for these strips, because they can be added wherever you like. Have fun with them and be creative, keeping in mind the following suggestions: Vary the length of your strips considerably— make them denser in some parts, less dense in others. By working these from the wrong side, an interesting variation in texture is created on the right side. Carry the main color along back when working these strips. When finishing a strip, give the main color yarns a firm tug before continuing the row.

To change color, complete last stitch of first color with next color. When working with B/C, drop A to wrong side to be picked up later in row, fasten off B when no longer needed for 3-double crochet block.

Row 6: With A/C, ch 2, hdc in each st across, changing to D for random sections of contrasting strips in row, turn (151 [159, 167] sts).

Rows 7-8: Rep rows 5-6, varying position and length of contrasting strips of D in Row 8.

Row 9: Ch 3, working in pattern of Row 3, positioning blocks of B/C over those in Row 3, dc in each of next 35 (37, 39) sts, dc3tog in next 3 sts, dc in each of next 73 (77, 81) sts, dc3tog in next 3 sts, dc in each of last 36 (38, 40) sts, turn (149 [157, 165] sts; 5 blocks of 3 dc in B/C evenly spaced across row).

Begin Arm Slit

Note: Rows where strips of D can be added are indicated, but it is not necessary to do so in each of the three sections now being worked.

Left Side

Row 10 (WS): Ch 3, dc in each of first 24 (26, 28) sts, turn (25 [27, 29] sts).

Row 11: Ch 2, hdc in each st across, turn (25 [27, 29] sts).

Row 12: Rep Row 11, adding D where desired.

Rows 13-14: Rep Rows 11-12 (25 [27, 29] sts).

Row 15: Ch 3, dc in each of next 13 sts, change to B/C, dc in each of next 3 sts, change to A/C, dc in each of last 8 (10, 12) sts, turn (25 [27, 29] sts; 1 block of B/C made).

Row 16: Ch 3, dc in each st across, turn (25 [27, 29] sts).

Rows 17–20: Rep Rows 11–14. Fasten off.

Pattern

Starting at bottom edge, with K–10 ½ hook, use one strand each of A and C held tog. Ch 153 (161, 169).

Row 1 (RS): Hdc in 3rd ch from hook and in each ch across, turn (151 [159, 167] sts).

Row 2: Ch 2, hdc in each st across, turn (151 [159, 167] sts).

Row 3: Ch 3, dc in each of next 7 (9, 11) hdc, *change to 1 strand each of B/C, dc in each of next 3 sts, change to A/C, dc in each of next 30 (31, 32) sts; rep from * (3 times), change to B/C, dc in each of next 3 sts, change to A/C, dc in each of last 8 (10, 12) sts, ch 3, turn (151 [159, 167] sts; 5 blocks of 3 dc in B/C evenly spaced across row).

Row 4: Ch 3, dc in each of next 24 (26, 28) dc, *change to B/C, dc in each of next 3 sts, change to A/C, dc in each of next 30 (31, 32) sts; rep from * twice, change to B/C, dc in each of next 3 sts, change to A/C, dc in each of next 24 (26, 28) sts, turn (151 [159, 167] sts; 4 blocks of 3 dc in B/C evenly spaced across row).

Row 5: With A/C, ch 2, hdc in each st across, turn (151 [159, 167] sts).

Back

Row 10: With WS facing, skip 1st st to the left of last st made in Row 10 of Left Side, with K-10 1/2 hook, join A/C in next st, ch 3, dc in each of next 96 (100, 104) sts, working two 3-dc blocks of B/C directly over blocks in Row 4, turn (97 [101, 105] sts; 2 blocks of B/C made).

Row 11: Ch 2, hdc in each of next 7 sts, hdc2tog (twice), hdc in each of next 73 (77, 81) sts, hdc2tog (twice), hdc in each of last 8 hdc, turn (93 [97, 101] sts).

Row 12: Ch 2 hdc in each st across, adding C where desired, turn (93 [97, 101] sts).

Row 13: Ch 2, hdc in each of next 6 sts, hdc2tog (twice), hdc in each of next 71 (75, 79) sts, hdc2tog (twice), hdc in each of last 7 sts, turn (91 [95, 99] sts).

Row 14: Rep Row 12 (91 [95, 99] sts).

Row 15: Maintaining position of B/C blocks in Row 3, ch 3, dc in each of next 6 sts, dc3tog in next 3 sts, dc in each st across to last 10 sts, dc3tog in next 3 sts, dc in each of last 7 sts, turn (87 [91, 95] sts).

Row 16: Maintaining position of B/C blocks in Row 4, ch 3, dc in each st across, turn (87 [91, 95] sts).

Row 17: Ch 2, hdc in each of next 4 sts, hdc2tog (twice), hdc in each st across to last 9 sts, hdc2tog (twice), hdc in each of last 5 sts, turn (83 [87, 91] sts).

Row 18: Rep Row 12 (83 [87, 91] sts).

Row 19: Ch 2, hdc in each of next 3 sts, hdc2tog (twice), hdc in each st across to last 8 sts, hdc2tog (twice), hdc in each of last 4 sts, turn (79 [83, 87] sts).

Row 20: Rep Row 12 (79 [83, 87] sts). Fasten off (81 [85, 89] sts).

Right Side

Row 10: With WS facing, skip 1st st to the left of last st made in Row 10 of Back, with K-10 ½ hook, join A/C in next st, ch 3, dc in each st across to side edge, turn (25 [27, 29] sts).

Rows 11–14: Rep Rows 11–14 of Left Side (25 [27, 29] sts).

Row 15: Ch 3, dc in each of next 7 (9, 11) sts, change to B/C, dc in each of next 3 sts, change to A/C, dc in each of last 14 sts, turn (25 [27, 29] sts; 1 block made).

Rows 16–20: Rep Rows 16–20 of Left Side (25 [27, 29] sts). Do not fasten off.

Join Sides and Back

Row 21 (joining row): With A/C, maintaining position of B/C blocks as in Row 3, ch 3, dc in st across RS to last st, dc2tog worked across last st on Right Side and first st on Back, dc in each of next 2 sts, dc3tog in next 3 sts, dc in each st across to last 6 sts of Back, dc3tog in next 3 sts, dc in each of next 2 sts, dc2tog in last st of Back and first st of left side, dc in each st across, turn (123 [131, 139] sts).

Row 22: Ch 3, maintaining position of B/C blocks as in Row 4, dc in each st across, turn (123 [131, 139] sts).

Row 23: Ch 2, hdc in each of next 25 (27, 29) sts, hdc2tog (twice), place a marker between last 2 decs, hdc in each of next 65(69, 73) sts, hdc2tog (twice), place a marker between last 2 decs, hdc in each of last 26 (28, 29) sts, turn (119 [127, 135] sts). Move markers up as work progresses.

Row 24: Ch 2 hdc in each st across, adding C where desired, turn (119 [127, 135] sts).

Row 25: Ch 2, hdc in each st across, working hdc2tog on each side of each marker (4 decs made), turn (115 [123, 131] sts).

Row 26: Rep Row 24 (115 [123, 131] sts).

Row 27: Ch 3, maintaining position of B/C blocks as in Row 3, dc in each st across, working dc3tog across 3 sts over each marker, turn (111 [119, 127] sts).

Row 28: Ch 3, maintaining position of B/C blocks as in Row 4, dc in each st across, turn (111 [119, 127] sts).

Row 29-40: Rep Row 23-28 (twice) (87 [95, 103] sts at end of Row 40).

Shape Neckline

Row 41: Sl st to 7th st, ch 2, hdc in each of next 11 (13, 15) sts, dc3tog (twice), (hdc in each of next 3 sts, hdc2tog) 7 (8, 9) times, hdc in each of next 3 sts, dc3tog (twice), hdc in each of next 12 (14, 16) sts, turn leaving rem sts unworked, turn (59 [67, 75] sts).

Sizes Small and Medium Only

Row 42: Ch 2, skip next hdc, hdc in each of next 8 (10) sts, dc3tog (twice), (hdc in each of next 2 sts, hdc2tog) 6 (7) times, hdc in each of next 3 sts, dc3tog (twice), hdc in each of next 8 (10) sts, skip next hdc, hdc in last st, turn (43 [50] sts).

Size Large Only

Row 42: Ch 1, sl st to 4th st, ch 2, skip next 2 hdc, hdc in each of next 8 sts, dc3tog (twice), (hdc in each of next 2 sts, hdc2tog) 8 times, hdc in each of next 3 sts, dc3tog (twice), hdc in each of next 8 sts, skip

next 2 hdc, hdc in next st, turn leaving rem sts unworked (49 sts).

All Sizes

Shoulders are now worked separately.

First Shoulder

Row 43: Ch 2, skip next 1 (2, 2) sts, dc3tog (twice), dc2tog (1 [1, 2] times), dc3tog (twice), skip next st, hdc in next st, turn (7 [7, 8] sts).

Row 44: Ch 2, dc2tog (dc2tog, dc3tog), dc3tog, hdc in last st (4 sts). Fasten off.

Second Shoulder

Row 43: With RS facing, skip 7 (8, 9) sts from last st made in Row 43 of First Shoulder, join A/C in next st, ch 2, skip next st, dc3tog (twice), dc2tog (1 [1, 2] times), dc3tog (twice), skip next 1 (2, 2) sts, hdc in last st, turn (7 [7, 8] sts).

Row 44: Ch 2, dc3tog (1 [1, 2] times, dc2tog (1 [1, 0] times, hdc in last st (4 sts). Fasten off.

Collar/Scarf

With RS of Poncho facing, using J-10 hook, join 1 strand each of C and E held tog in top right-hand corner of neck edge (last st in Row 40), ch 85.

Row 1: Hdc in 3rd ch from hook, hdc in each ch across to neck edge, work 23 (23, 25) hdc evenly across shoulder shaping to first skipped st in center section of Row 42, 2 hdc in each st across back neck edge, 23 (23, 25) hdc evenly across other side of shoulder shaping to top left-hand corner of Row 40, turn (60 [62, 68] sts for collar; 84 sts for scarf).

Row 2: Ch 2, hdc in each of next 15 (17, 19) sts, hdc2tog (4 times), 3 hdc, hdc2tog (3 times), 3 hdc, hdc2tog (4 times), hdc in each of next 16 (18, 20) sts on Collar, hdc in each st across Scarf, turn (49 [51, 57] sts for Collar; 84 sts for Scarf).

Row 3: Ch 2, hdc in each of next 83 sts for Scarf, hdc in each of next 11 (12, 15) sts of Collar, hdc2tog, (hdc in each of next 3 sts, hdc2tog,) 5 times, hdc in each of last 11 (12, 15) (44 [46, 52] sts for collar; 84 sts for scarf)

Rows 4–7: Ch 2, hdc in each st across Collar and Scarf. Fasten off. Weave in all ends.

Border

Row 1: With RS of Poncho facing, using J-10 hook, join 2 strands of F in top left-hand corner at base of Collar, ch 1, sc evenly across side edge, 4 sc in corner st, sc evenly across bottom edge, 4 sc in next corner st, sc evenly across other side edge to base of Scarf, turn.

Rows 2–3: Ch 1, sc in each sc across, working 4 sc in each corner, turn. Fasten off.

Bottom Trim: With RS facing, using J-10 hook, join 2 strands of F in bottom left-hand corner st, ch 1, sc in each st across bottom edge. Fasten off. Weave in ends.

Hand Slit Trim

With RS facing, using J-10 hook, join 1 strand each of B and C in bottom of 1 Hand Slit opening, sl st evenly around, sl st in first sl st to join. Rep around other hand slit.

THIS PROJECT WAS CREATED WITH 5 skeins of Lion Brand *Wool-Ease* in Mushroom (#403), 10% wool/86% acrylic/4% rayon, 3oz/85g = 197yd/180m

1 skein of Cervinia *Sorrento* in Charcoal, 100% acrylic, 1 ¾ oz/50 gr = 100 yd/91m

2 skeins of Cervinia *Fiamma* in variegated yellows/browns, 70% acrylic/30% merino, 3 ½ oz/100 gr = 104yd/95m

3 balls of Lion Brand *Fun Fur* in Lava (#204), 100% polyester, 1 ½oz/40g = 57yd/52m

This rugged poncho is a clever interpretation of a classic Aran knit fisherman's sweater—with a twist. You won't find fringe on a fisherman's sweater as he heads out on the high seas.

CABLED ARAN PONCHO • *Designed by Laura Gebhardt*

SKILL LEVEL: INTERMEDIATE

FINISHED MEASUREMENT
One size fits most
Back: 42" wide x 22" long/107 x 56cm excluding fringe
Front: 42" wide x 18" long/107 x 46cm excluding fringe

YOU WILL NEED
1872yd/1711m worsted weight yarn
Hook: size 5.5mm/I–9 or size needed to obtain gauge
Yarn needle

STITCHES USED
Chain stitch (ch)
Double crochet (dc)
Single crochet (sc)
Slip stitch (sl st)

SPECIAL STITCH TECHNIQUES
Bobble: (Yo, insert hook in st, yo, draw yarn through st, yo, draw yarn through 2 loops on hook) 4 times in same st, yo, draw yarn through 5 loops on hook.
Front post double crochet (fpdc): Yo, insert hook from front to back to front again, around the post of designated st, yo, draw yarn through st and up to level of current row, (yo, draw yarn through 2 loops on hook) twice.
Back post double crochet (bpdc): Yo, insert hook from back to front to back again, around the post of designated st, yo, draw yarn through st and up to level of current row, (yo, draw yarn through 2 loops on hook) twice.

GAUGE
Take time to check your gauge.
14 sts and 16 rows in back pattern = 4"/10cm

Back
Ch 146.

Row 1: Sc in 2nd ch from hook, sc in each ch across, turn (145 sc).

Row 2: Ch 1, sc in each sc across, turn (145 sc).

Row 3: Ch 1, sc in each of first 2 sc, *fpdc around the post of next corresponding sc 2 rows below, skip sc behind fpdc just made, sc in next sc, fpdc around the post of next corresponding sc 2 rows below, skip sc behind fpdc just made**, sc in each of next 3 sc; rep from * across ending last rep at **, sc in last 2 sc, turn (24 pairs of fpdc; 24 cables begun).

Row 4: Ch 1, sc in each of first 6 sts, *bobble in next sc, sc in next 5 sts; rep from * across to last sc, sc in last sc, turn (23 bobbles).

Row 5: Ch 1, sc in each of first 2 sc, *fpdc around the post of next corresponding fpdc 2

rows below, skip sc behind fpdc just made, sc in next sc, fpdc around the post of next corresponding fpdc 2 rows below, skip sc behind fpdc just made**, sc in each of next 3 sc; rep from * across to last 2 sts, ending last rep at **, sc in last 2 sc, turn (24 pairs of fpdc).

Row 6: Ch 1, sc in each st across (145 sc)

Row 7: Rep Row 5.

Row 8: Rep Row 4

Row 9 (twisted cables row): Ch 1, sc in each of first 2 sc, *skip next fpdc 2 rows below, fpdc around the post of next fpdc 2 rows below, skip sc behind fpdc just made, sc in next sc, working in front of previous fpdc, fpdc around the post of skipped fpdc to the left 2 rows below, skip sc behind fpdc just made**, sc in each of next 3 sc, rep from * across to last 2 sts, ending last rep at **, sc in last 2 sc.

Row 10: Rep Row 6

Row 11: Rep Row 5.

Rows 12–83: Rep Rows 4-11 (9 times).

Rows 84–87: Rep Rows 4-7. Fasten off.

Front

Work same as back through Row 63.

Shape Neck and Right Shoulder

Row 64 (WS): Ch 1, sc in each of first 65 sts, sc2tog in next 2 sts, turn, leaving rem sts unworked (66 sts)

Row 65: Ch 1, sc2tog in first 2 sts, work in established pattern across, turn (65 sts).

Row 66: Work in established pattern across to last 2 sts, sc2tog in last 2 sts, turn (64 sts).

Rows 67–70: Maintaining established pattern, rep Rows 65-66 (twice) (60 sts at end of last row)

Row 71: Work even in established pattern across (60 sts). Fasten off.

Left Shoulder

Row 64: With WS facing, skip next 11 sts to the left of last st made in Row 64 of Right Shoulder, join yarn in next st, ch 1, sc2tog in first 2 sts, sc in each st across, turn (66 sts).

Row 65: Work in established pattern across to last 2 sts, sc2tog in last 2 sts, turn (65 sts).

Row 66: Ch 1, sc2tog in first 2 sts, work in established pattern across, turn (64 sts).

Rows 67–70: Maintaining established pattern, rep Rows 65-66 (twice) (60 sts at end of last row).

Row 71: Work even in established pattern across (60 sts). Fasten off.

Assembly

Face right sides together. Use a yarn needle to sew front to back at shoulders.

Neck Band

Rnd 1: With RS of poncho facing, join yarn in 1st st to the left of shoulder seam on back neck edge, ch 3, dc in each of next 24 sts across back neck, working in row-end sts, work 11 dc evenly spaced down left neck shaping, dc in each of next 11 dc across front neck edge, work 11 dc evenly spaced up right neck shaping. Sl st in 3rd ch of turning ch (58 dc).

Rnd 2: Ch 2, *fpdc around the post of next dc, bpdc around the post of next dc; rep from * around. Sl st in 2nd ch of turning ch (58 sts)

Rnd 3: Ch 2, *fpdc around the post of next fpdc, bpdc around the post of next bpdc; rep from * around. Sl st in 2nd ch of turning ch (58 sts). Fasten off.

Side Edgings

With RS facing, join yarn in side of 1st st made in Row 1 of back, ch 1, sc evenly up edge to shoulder seam and down edge to bottom Front corner. Rep for other side edge beg at bottom Front and working to bottom Back corner. Fasten off. Weave in ends.

Fringe

Cut 13"/33cm lengths of yarn. Using 2 lengths for each fringe, knot one fringe in every other stitch across bottom edges of front and back.

Fold strands in half. Insert hook in loop, put folded strands over hook pulling through slightly. With folded strand remaining on hook, yo and pull yarn ends through fold. Trim ends even.

THIS PROJECT WAS CREATED WITH 6 skeins of TLC *Essentials* in Aran (#2313), 100% acrylic, 6 oz/170g = 312yd/285m

This fabulous textured poncho makes any outfit even more special. Puff stitches and double crochets paired with a thick and thin textured yarn, spin an intricate, rich fabric. Add bold fringe to the asymmetrical shape to create even more drama.

DULCE PONCHO • *Designed by Katherine Lee*

SKILL LEVEL: INTERMEDIATE

FINISHED MEASUREMENTS
One size fits most
Neck edge: 27"/69cm in circumference
Length: 28"/71cm from neck edge to center front point

YOU WILL NEED
598yd/547m bulky weight yarn
Hook: size 9mm/M–13 or size to obtain gauge
Yarn needle

STITCHES USED
Chain stitch (ch)
Double crochet (dc)
Single crochet (sc)
Treble crochet (tr)

SPECIAL STITCH TECHNIQUE
Puff stitch (puff st): Yo, insert hook in next st, yo, draw through a lp 3 times. Yo, draw through all 7 lps on hook, ch 1, tightly to close puff stitch.

GAUGE
Take time to check your gauge. One pattern rep = 3 ¾"/10cm measured from the base of one pair of puff sts to the next pair of puff sts; 4 rows in pattern = 3 ¾"/10cm

Front

Ch 63.

Row 1: Puff st in 7th ch from hook, *ch 3, skip next 3 ch, sc in next ch, ch 3, skip next 3 ch, (puff st, ch 4, puff st) in next ch; rep from * to across, ending last rep with (puff st, ch 2, tr) in last ch, turn.

Row 2: Ch 1, sc in tr, *ch 2, skip next 2 sps, 3 dc in next sc, ch 2, skip next ch-3 sp, sc in next ch-4 loop; rep from * across, ending last rep with sc in last ch-6 loop, turn.

Row 3: Ch 1, sc in 1st sc, *ch 3, skip next dc, (puff st, ch 4, puff st) in next dc, ch 3, skip next ch-2 sp, sc in next sc; rep from * across, turn.

Row 4: Ch 3, dc in 1st sc, *ch 2, skip next ch-3 sp, sc in next ch-4 loop, ch 2, skip next ch-3 sp, 3 dc in next sc; rep from * across, ending last rep with 2 dc in last sc, turn.

Row 5: Ch 6, puff st in 1st dc, *ch 3, skip next ch-2 sp, sc in next sc, ch 3, skip next dc, (puff st, ch 4, puff st) in next dc; rep from * across, ending last rep with (puff st, ch 2, tr) in 3rd ch of turning ch, turn.

Rows 6–17: Rep Rows 2–5 (3 times).

Rows 18–20: Rep Rows 2–4.

Shape Neck

Row 21 (dec row): Ch 6, puff st in 1st dc, *ch 3, skip next ch-2 sp, sc in next sc, ch 3, skip next dc, (puff st, ch 4, puff st) in next dc; rep from * across, ending with sc in last sc, turn, leaving rem sts unworked.

Row 22: Ch 3, dc in 1st sc, *ch 2, skip next ch-3 sp, sc in next ch-4 loop, ch 2, skip next ch-3 sp, 3 dc in next sc; rep from * across to last 2 loops, ch 2, skip next ch-3 sp, sc in last ch-6 loop, turn.

Row 23 (dec row): Rep Row 3 across to last sc, turn, leaving rem sts unworked.

Row 24: Rep Row 4.

Row 25 (dec row): Rep Row 5 across, ending with puff st in 3rd ch of turning ch, turn.

Row 26: Ch 1, sc in 1st puff st, *ch 2, skip next 2 sps, 3 dc in next sc, ch 2, skip next ch-3 sp, sc in next ch-4 loop; rep from * across, ending last rep with sc in last ch-6 loop, turn.

Rows 27–29: Rep Rows 3–5.

Rows 30–33: Rep Rows 2–5.

Rows 34–36: Rep Rows 2–4. Fasten off.

Back

Work same as Front through Row 35.

Row 36 (joining row): With back and front facing, matching sts, ch 3, sl st to corresponding corner st of front, dc in 1st sc on back, *ch 2, sl st to next sc on front, sc in next ch-4 loop on back, ch 2, dc in next sc, skip next dc on front, sl st in next dc on front, dc in same sc on back as last dc; rep from * across, ending last rep with dc in last sc on back, sl st in 3rd ch of turning ch on front. Fasten off.

Finishing

Weave in ends. Lightly block poncho to even out stitches. Sew front to back along side edges.

Fringe

Cut 18"/46cm lengths of yarn for fringe. Using 3 strands for each fringe, attach 1 fringe in chain at the base of each puff stitch pair along bottom edge as follows: Fold strands in half. Insert hook in chain, put folded strands over hook pulling through slightly. With folded strand remaining on hook, yarn over and pull yarn ends through fold.

THIS PROJECT WAS CREATED WITH 13 balls of Katia Yarns *Dulce Plus* in Green (#56), 50% wool/50% acrylic, 1 ¾oz/50g = 46yd/42m

SKILL LEVEL: INTERMEDIATE

FINISHED MEASUREMENTS
One size fits most
*V-neck to longest point
approx: 27"/69cm*
*Arm to hem: approx
18"/46cm.*

YOU WILL NEED
Approx 459yd/420m bulky
weight yarn
Approx 370yd/338m bulky
weight nubby yarn
Approx 250yd/229m bulky
weight bouclé yarn
Hook: 9mm/N-13 and
6.5mm/K–10 ½ or size
needed to obtain gauge
Stitch markers (optional)
7"/18cm piece of card-
board for winding fringe

STITCHES USED
Chain stitch st (ch)
Single crochet (sc)
Double crochet (dc)

SPECIAL STITCH TECHNIQUES
V-stitch (V-st): 2 dc in indicated st or sp. (This V-st
has no ch 1 between the
dcs and is an abbreviated
form of the usual V-st.)
*Double crochet decrease
(dc2tog):* (Yo, insert hook in
next st, yo, draw yarn
through st, yo, draw yarn
through 2 loops on hook)
twice, yo, draw yarn
through 3 loops on hook.
*Single crochet decrease
(sc2tog):* (Insert hook in
next st, yo, draw yarn
through st) twice, yo, draw
yarn through 3 loops on
hook.

GAUGE
*Take time to check
your gauge.*
With N–13 hook and A,
10 sts and 4 rows =
4"/10cm in dc.
With K–10½ hook and B,
10 sts and 5 rows =
4"/10cm in dc.

BLUE-STRIPED PONCHO • *Designed by Donna Hulka*

This classically shaped poncho in simple alternating strips is the perfect opportunity for you to play with a custom-designed color palatte.

Main Section

With N-13 hook and A, ch 128.

Row 1 (RS): Working into both top loops of ch, sc in 2nd ch from hook, *ch 1, skip next ch, sc in next ch; rep from * across, turn (127 sts; 63 ch-1 sps).

Row 2: Ch 3, V-st in 1st ch-1 sp, V-st in each ch-1 sp across, ending with dc in last ch-1 sp, dc in last sc (counts as V-st), turn (127 sts).

Row 3: Ch 1, sc in 1st dc, ch 1, sc in sp between next dc and next V-st, *ch 1, sc in sp between next 2 V-sts; rep from * across, ending with ch 1, sc in sp bet last V-st and beg ch-3, changing to B in last sc, turn (127 sts; 63 ch-1 sps).

Row 4: K-10½ hook and B, ch 3, V-st in each ch-1 sp across, ending with dc in last ch-1 sp, dc in last sc, changing to yarn C in last dc, turn (127 sts).

Row 5: With C, ch 3, skip 1st dc, V-st in sp bet next dc and next V-st, (V-st in sp bet next 2 V-st) across, ending with V-st in sp bet last V-st and beg ch-3, changing to B in last dc, turn (127 sts).

Row 6: With B, rep Row 5, changing to A in last dc, turn (127 sts).

Row 7: With N-13 hook and A, rep Row 3.

Row 8: Ch 3, (dc, ch 1) in each ch-1 sp across to last ch-1 sp, dc in last ch-1 sp, dc in last sc, turn, (127 sts).

Row 9: Ch 3, dc in next dc, (ch 1, dc) in each ch-1 sp across, ending with dc in next dc, dc in top of beg ch-3, turn (127 sts).

Row 10: Ch 1, sc in 1st 2 dc, ch 1, skip next dc, (sc, ch 1) in each ch-1 sp across, skip next dc, sc in next dc, sc in top of beg ch-3, changing to C in last sc, turn (127 sts).

Row 11: K-10½ hook and C, ch 3, dc in 1st dc, V-st in each ch-1 sp across, ending with 1 dc in last sc, changing to A in last dc, turn (127 sts).

Row 12: With N-13 hook and A, ch 1, sc in 1st dc, *ch 1, sc in sp bet next 2 V-sts; rep from * across, ending with ch 1, sc in top of beg ch-3, turn (127 sts; 63 ch-1 sps).

Row 13–21: Rep Rows 2–10.

Row 22: With K-10 1/2 hook and C, ch 3, dc in next sc, *V-st in each of next 5 ch-1 sps, dc2tog over next 2 ch-1 sp; rep from * 7 times, V-st in each of next 6 ch-1 sps, dc in last sc, changing to A in last dc, turn (103 sts).

Row 23: With N-13 hook and A, ch 1, sc in 1st dc, *ch 1, sc in sp bet next 2 V-sts or between V-st and dc2tog; rep from * across, ending with ch 1, sc in top of beg ch-3, turn (111 sts; 55 ch-1 sps).

Row 24–32: Rep Rows 2–10 (111 sts). Fasten off.

Side Section

With N-13 hook and A, ch 34.

Rows 1–21: Rep Rows 1–21 of Main Section (33 sts).

Row 22: With K-10½ hook and C, ch 3, dc in 1st dc, (V-st in next ch-1 sp) across, working 2 dc2tog decs evenly spaced within the row (27 sts). Fasten off.

Assembly

Fold both main and side sections in half, with right sides facing. Row 1 on each (the longer side) goes at the neckline. Lay out pieces as shown. Sew sections together at seams.

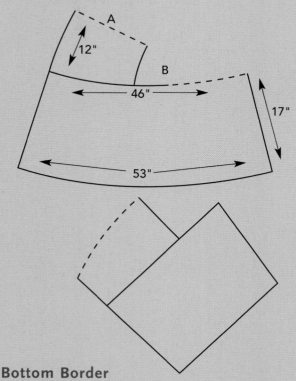

Bottom Border

With RS facing, using N-13 hook, join A in any ch-1 sp, ch 1, (sc, ch 1) in each ch-1 sp around, working (sc, ch 1, sc) in same st at front and back points, sl st to 1st sc to join. Fasten off.

Neck Border

Rnd 1: With RS facing, using K–10½ hook, join A in any ch-1 sp (except not at point of V-neck), ch 1, sc in each sc and each ch-1 sp around, working sc2tog dec at front and back points of V-neck, sl st to 1st sc to join.

Rnd 2: Ch 1, sc in each sc around, working sc2tog dec at front and back points of V-neck, sl st to 1st sc to join. Fasten off.

Fringe

Use a 7"/18cm square of cardboard to wrap and cut enough 14"/35.6 cm pieces of yarns A, B, and C for each ch-1 sp around bottom border. Cut the wrapped yarns along the bottom edge of the cardboard. Attach fringe in ch-1 sps, incorporating any unworked ends into fringe. Trim fringe evenly to desired length.

> **THIS PROJECT WAS CREATED WITH** 3 skeins of Lion Brand *Wool-Ease Chunky* in Bay Harbor (#115), 80% acrylic/20% wool, 5oz/140g = 153yd/140m
>
> 2 skeins of Lion Brand *Homespun* in Williamsburg (#312), 98% acrylic/2% polyester, 6oz/170g = 185yd/169m
>
> 2 skeins of Lion Brand *Color Waves* in Caribbean (#307), 83% acrylic/17% polyester, 3oz/85g = 125yd/113m

SKILL LEVEL: INTERMEDIATE

FINISHED MEASUREMENTS
One size fits most
Neck edge: 23"/58cm
circumference
Bottom edge: 55"/140cm
circumference
Length: 19"/48cm from shoulder to
bottom edge

YOU WILL NEED
Approx 755yd/690m DK weight
mohair blend yarn
Hook: size 7mm/K/10½ or size
needed to obtain gauge
Yarn needle
1"/2.5cm pin back (optional)

STITCHES USED
Chain stitch (ch)
Double crochet (dc)
Slip stitch (sl st)

SPECIAL STITCH
V-stitch (V-st): 2 dc in same st or sp

GAUGE
*Take time to check
your gauge.*
One pattern rep (19 sts) in scallop
pattern = 5½"/14cm; 4 rows in scallop pattern = 3"/8cm; 13 sts and 6
rows dc = 4"/10cm.

LIGHT AS A LACY FEATHER ● *Designed by Katherine Lee*

The featherweight feel of luxurious super
kid mohair inspired this lacy cowl neck
poncho. It's crocheted using a fairly large
size K hook so the soft fibers of the yarn
can come through. The scalloped lacy
border is an elegant finish.

Front/Back (make 2)

Beg on bottom edge, ch 98.

Row 1: 5 dc in 4th ch from hook, (sk next ch, dc in next ch) 3 times, sk next ch, dc2tog worked across next 3 ch, (sk next ch, dc in next ch) 3 times, *sk next ch, 6 dc in each of next 2 ch, (sk next ch, dc in next ch) 3 times, sk next ch, dc2tog worked across next 3 ch, (sk next ch, dc in next ch) 3 times; rep from * across to last 2 ch, sk 1 ch, 6 dc in last ch, turn (95 sts).

Row 2: Ch 3, 5 dc in 1st dc, (sk next dc, 1 dc in next dc) 3 times, sk next dc, dc2tog worked across next 3 dc, (sk next dc, dc in next dc) 3 times, *sk 1 st, 6 dc in each of next 2 sts, (sk next dc, dc in next dc) 3 times, sk next dc, dc2tog worked across next 3 dc, (sk next dc, dc in next dc) 3 times; rep from * across to last 2 sts, sk next dc, 6 dc in 3rd ch of tch, turn (95 sts).

Row 3–4: Rep Row 2.

Row 5: Ch 4 (counts as dc, ch 1), sk next dc, *dc in next dc, ch 1, sk next dc; rep from * across, ending with dc in 3rd ch of tch, turn (47 ch-1 sps).

Row 6: Ch 3, dc in 1st ch-1 sp (counts as first V-st), V-st in each ch-1 sp across, ending with dc in last ch-1 sp, dc in 3rd ch of tch (counts as last V-st), turn (47 V-sts).

Row 7: Ch 3, skip next 2 dc, dc bet last skipped and next dc, ch 1, (dc, ch 1) in space between next 2 V-sts; rep from * across to last 4 sts, dc in space bet next V-st and next dc, dc in 3rd ch of tch, turn (45 ch-1 sps).

Rows 8–27: Rep Rows 6–7 (10 times) (25 ch-1 sps at end of Row 27)

Row 28: Rep Row 6 (25 V-sts). Fasten off.

Assembly

Very gently steam poncho to flatten scalloped edge. With right sides facing, match stitches. Use a yarn needle to sew front to back along side edges starting above scalloped edge, working across side edge, and in the first 10 stitches across top edge of last row for shoulders.

Cowl neck

Rnd 1: With RS of Front facing, join yarn in left shoulder seam on neck edge, ch 4 (counts as dc, ch 1), *(dc, ch 1) between next 2 V-sts*; rep from * to * across to next shoulder seam, (dc, ch 1) in shoulder seam, rep from * to * around. Sl st in 3rd ch of turning ch to join (30 ch-1 sps).

Rnd 2: Sl st in 1st ch-1 sp, ch 3, dc in same ch-1 sp, V-st in each ch-1 sp around. Sl st in 3rd ch of turning ch to join (30 V-sts).

Rnd 3: Ch 4 (counts as dc), ch 1, *(dc, ch 1) bet next 2 V-sts; rep from * around. Sl st in 3rd ch of turning ch to join (30 ch-1 sps).

Rnds 4–5: Rep Rnd 2–3.

Rnd 6: Rep Rnd 2.

Rnd 7 (Inc rnd): Ch 4, dc in sp bet ch-3 and 1st dc, ch 1 (inc made), *(dc, ch 1) bet next 2 V-sts*; rep from * to * 14 times, (dc, ch 1, dc, ch 1) in sp bet next V-st (inc made), rep from * to * around (32 ch-1 sps). Place a marker in each inc sp, move markers up as work progresses.

Rnds 8–9: Rep Rnd 2–3

Rnd 10: Rep Rnd 2.

Rnd 11 (Inc rnd): Ch 4, dc in sp bet ch-3 and 1st dc, ch 1 (inc made), *(dc, ch 1) bet next 2 V-sts*; rep from * to * to next marked sp, (dc, ch 1, dc, ch 1) in next marked sp (inc made), rep from * to * around (34 ch-1 sps).

Rnds 12-13: Rep Rnd 2-3.

Rnd 14: Rep Rnd 2. Fasten off.

Crocheted Flower

Wind yarn around fingers several times. Remove loop from fingers and fasten with a slip stitch.

Rnd 1: Ch 1, 18 sc in ring. Sl st in first sc to join (18 sc).

Rnd 2: Ch 6, sk first 3 sc, *hdc in next sc, ch 4, sk next 2 sc; rep from * around. Sl st in first sc to join (6 ch-4 loops).

Rnd 3: Ch 1, (sc, hdc, 3 dc, hdc, sc) in each ch-4 loop around. Sl st in first sc to join (6 petals).

Rnd 4: Sl st into back of corresponding hdc in Rnd 2, *ch 5, working in back of petals, sl st into back of next hdc in Rnd 2; rep from * around, ending with sl st in first hdc (6 ch-5 loops)

Rnd 5: Ch 1, (sc, hdc, 5 dc, hdc, sc) in each ch-5 lp around. Sl st in first sc to join (6 petals).

Rnd 6: Sl st into back of corresponding sl st in Rnd 4, *ch 6, working in back of petals, sl st into back of next sl st in Rnd 4; rep from * around, ending with sl st in first hdc (6 ch-6 loops).

Rnd 7: Ch 1, (sc, hdc, 7 dc, hdc, sc) in each ch-6 lp around. Sl st in first sc to join (6 petals). Fasten off.

Sew to pin back or sew directly to front of poncho as desired.

Weave in ends.

THIS PROJECT WAS CREATED WITH 5 balls of GGH *Soft Kid* in Lilac (#13), 70% Super Kid Mohair/25% Nylon/5% Wool, .875oz/25g = 151yd/138m

SKILL LEVEL: INTERMEDIATE

FINISHED MEASUREMENTS
One size fits most
Width: 51"/129cm
Length: 27"/69cm from neck edge to bottom edge

YOU WILL NEED
Approx 2900yd/2651m worsted weight wool (A)
Approx 170yd/155m bulky weight yarn (B)
Approx 225yd/206m worsted weight mohair yarn in same color as B (C)
Hook *(body)*: size 5.5mm/I–9 or size needed to obtain gauge
Hook *(trim)*: size 4.25mm/G–6 or size needed to obtain gauge
Yarn needle

STITCHES USED
Chain stitch (ch)
Double crochet (dc)
Half double crochet (hdc)
Single crochet (sc)
Treble crochet (tr)

SPECIAL STITCH TECHNIQUES
Front post double crochet (fpdc): Yo, insert hook from front to back to front again, around the post of designated st, yo, draw yarn through st and up to level of current row, (yo, draw yarn through 2 loops on hook) twice.

Back post double crochet (bpdc): Yo, insert hook from back to front to back again, around the post of designated st, yo, draw yarn through st and up to level of current row, (yo, draw yarn through 2 loops on hook) twice.

Back post half double crochet (bphdc): Yo, insert hook from back to front to back again, around the post of designated st, yo, draw yarn through st and up to level of current row, yo, draw yarn through 3 loops on hook.

GAUGE
Take time to check your gauge.
(Sc, ch 2) 6 times and 12 rows in pattern = 4"/10cm

STAIR STEPS TO HEAVEN PONCHO • *Designed by Linda Buckner*

Hand painted yarns are a luxurious choice for knitting and crochet. Add the interesting edge treatment to this poncho and you're on your way to . . . you know where.

For the handwoven look of this poncho, 2 strands of A (worsted weight yarn) are worked over 1 strand of B yarn (thick yarn). On every row, lay the thick strand along the top of the underlying row and crochet by inserting the hook under the thick strand. The thicker strand is wrapped around the end when turning the work, so it is continuous throughout the piece. Be sure to keep the row straight and laying flat (don't bunch up the thicker yarn or pull too tight) by smoothing each row as you work. The method is similar to crocheting over ends.

The poncho is reversible. It can also be worked with B worked over 2 strands of A for a different look.

Transform this poncho into an unusual pullover, if desired. Sew the second step from the neck and down the side as far as needed.

Front/Back (make 2)

Starting at top edge, with I-9 hook and 2 strands of A held together as one, ch 207, turn.

Row 1 (RS): Place strand of B across top of foundation ch, working over strand of B, sc in 3rd ch from hook, *ch 2, skip next 2 ch, sc in next ch; rep from * 67 times, sc in last ch, wrap B around end, turn (68 ch-2 sps).

Row 2: Ch 2 (counts as 1st sc), keeping B to the front and A to the back, * working over B, sc in next sc on previous row, ch 2, skip next ch-2 sp; rep from * across, sc in next sc, sc in turning ch, wrap B around end, turn (68 ch-2 sps).

Rows 3–11: Rep Row 2 (68 ch-2 sps). Fasten off A and B.

Row 12: With WS facing, skip first 4 ch-2 sps, skip next sc and next ch, lay B across top of previous row, join 2 strands A in next ch, ch 2, sc in next sc, ch 2, skip next ch-2 sp; rep from * across to within last 6 ch-2 sps, sc in next sc, sc in next ch, wrap B around end, turn (58 ch-2 sps).

Rows 13–22: Rep Row 2 (58 ch-2 sps). Fasten off A and B.

Rows 23–242: Rep Rows 12-22 (5 times) (8 ch-2 sps at end of Row 242). Fasten off.

First Shoulder Panel

Row 1 (WS): With WS of Front facing, working across opposite side of foundation ch, with G-6 hook and 2 strands of A held tog as one, join yarn in first ch, ch 3, hdc in each of next 78 ch, turn (79 sts). Fasten off A, join C.

Row 2 (RS): With C, ch 4, *skip the next 3 hdc, tr in each of next 3 hdc, working in back of the 3 tr just made, tr in each of the 3 skipped hdc; rep from * 12 times, tr in next hdc, turn (13 triangle groups made). Fasten off C, join 2 strands A.

Row 3: With 2 strands A, ch 3, hdc in each st, turn (79 sts).

Row 4: Rep Row 2 (79 sts). Fasten off A, join C.

Rows 5-6: Rep Rows 2-3. Fasten off C.

Second Shoulder Panel

Row 1 (WS): With WS of front facing, skip center 44 sts to the left of last st made in Row 1 of first shoulder panel (there should be 79 sts remaining to work second shoulder panel), with G-6 hook and 2 strands of A held together as one, join yarn in next ch, ch 3, hdc in each of next 78 ch, turn (79 sts). Fasten off A, join C.

Rows 2–6: Rep Rows 2-6 of First Shoulder Panel. Fasten off.

Repeat with shoulder panels on top edge of kack.

Assembly

With yarn needle and 2 strands A, sew front to back at shoulder seams.

Outer Edging

Rnd 1: With RS of Poncho facing, using I-9 hook, join 2 strands A in corner st of first step to the left of one shoulder seam, ch 3, hdc in the same space, *hdc in the sc, 2 hdc in next ch-2 sp; rep from * across to one st before next inside corner, yo, pull up a loop in next st, pull up a loop in corner st, pull up a loop in next st, yo, pull through all loops on hook (one corner dec made), work 8-10 hdc evenly spaced (work as many sts as needed to keep work laying flat) across row-end sts of next 11 rows, working over B strands and into A sts to secure B strands (this adds to the stability of the shape of the garment, preventing the homespun from pulling), work 3 hdc in corner st; rep from ** around entire garment, working hdc evenly spaced across shoulder panels. Sl st in 3rd ch of turning ch to join.

Neck Edging

Rnd 1: With WS of Poncho facing, using I-9 hook, join 2 strands A in first st to the left of First Shoulder panel, ch 3, *hdc evenly across neck edge, (working hdc in each sc and 2 hdc in each ch-2 sp) to one st before inside corner, work corner dec (same as on outer edging) across corner, work 16 hdc evenly spaced across shoulder panel to one st before next inside corner, work corner dec in next corner; rep from * around. Sl st in 3rd ch of turning ch to join.

Rnd 2: With G-6 hook, ch 3, hdc in each hdc around neck opening, working a corner dec in each inside corner. Sl st in 3rd ch of turning ch to join. Fasten off A, join C.

Rnd 3: With G-6 hook and C, rep Rnd 2. Fasten off C, join 2 strands A

Rnd 4: With 2 strands A, ch 3, bpdc around the post of each hdc around, working a corner dec in each inside corner as before. Sl st in 3rd ch of turning ch to join. Fasten off A, join C.

Rnd 5: With C, ch 3, bphdc around the post of each hdc around, working a corner dec in each inside corner as before. Sl st in 3rd ch of turning ch to join. Fasten off C, join 2 strands A.

Rnd 6: Rep Rnd 4. Fasten off.

Finishing

Weave in ends. Steam outer edges and neck opening, being careful not to place hot iron on stitches.

THIS PROJECT WAS CREATED WITH 2 skeins of Mountain Colors *Wool Crepe* in Indian Corn, 100% Merino wool, 12oz/336g = 1450yd/1326m

1 skein of Mountain Colors *Homespun* in Glacier Teal, 85% wool/15% silk, 7oz/200g = 170yd/155m

1 skein of Mountain Colors *Mohair* in Glacier Teal, 73% mohair/13% wool/9% nylon, 3½oz/100g = 225yd/206m

SKILL LEVEL: INTERMEDIATE

FINISHED MEASUREMENTS
One size fits most
Neck opening: 28"/71cm circumference
Length: 27"/69cm from V at neckline to center front point

YOU WILL NEED
960 yd/878m sport weight yarn
Hook: size 4mm/F-5 or size needed to obtain gauge
Yarn needle

STITCHES USED
Chain stitch (ch)
Double crochet (dc)
Single crochet (sc)
Slip stitch (sl st)

FILET CROCHET TERMS
Space: Dc in dc, ch 2, skip 2 sts, dc in next dc (to start next space or block).

Block when worked over space: Dc in dc, 2 dc in next ch-2 sp, dc in next dc (to start next space or block).
Block when worked over block: Dc in dc, dc in each of next 2 dc, dc in next dc (to start next space or block).
Lacet: Ch 2, skip next 2 sts, sc in next st, ch 2, skip next 2 sts, dc in next dc (to start next space or block).
Double space: Dc in dc, ch 5, skip next 5 sts, dc in next dc (to start next space or block).

GAUGE
Take time to check your gauge.
19 sts and 7 rows dc = 4"/10cm

MODERN VICTORIAN PONCHO • *Designed by Nanette Seale*

This filet crochet poncho is a modern interpretation of a classically Victorian technique. Wear it over a solid color to show off the intricate (but easy) pattern.

Large Rectangle

Ch 93.

Row 1: Dc in 4th ch from hook, dc in each ch across (30 blocks made – Row 1 of Chart A complete).

Rows 2–89: Work in blocks, spaces, double spaces and lacets following chart A. Fasten off at end of Row 89.

Small Rectangle

Ch 93.

Row 1: Dc in 4th ch from hook, dc in each ch across (30 blocks made – Row 1 of Chart B complete).

Rows 2-26: Work in blocks, spaces, double spaces and lacets following Chart B. Fasten off at end of Row 26.

Assembly

With yarn needle and yarn, sew the rectangles together, sewing last row of the small rectangle to row-end stitches of first 30 rows on side edge of large rectangle. Sew bottom edge of small rectangle to last 30 row-end sts on same side edge of large rectangle.

Neck edge

With right sides facing, attach yarn in one center V, ch 1, sc evenly around, working sc in side of each row, and sc base of each row. Sl st in first sc to join. Fasten off.

Border

Rnd 1: With RS facing, attach yarn in one bottom point, ch 1, sc evenly around, working 3 sc in each point. Sl st in first sc to join. Fasten off.

Rnd 2: Ch 3, (2 dc, ch 3, 3 dc) in same st (first shell made), *skip next 5 sts, (3 dc, ch 3, 3 dc) in next st, rep * around. Sl st in 3rd ch of turning ch to join. Fasten off. Weave in ends.

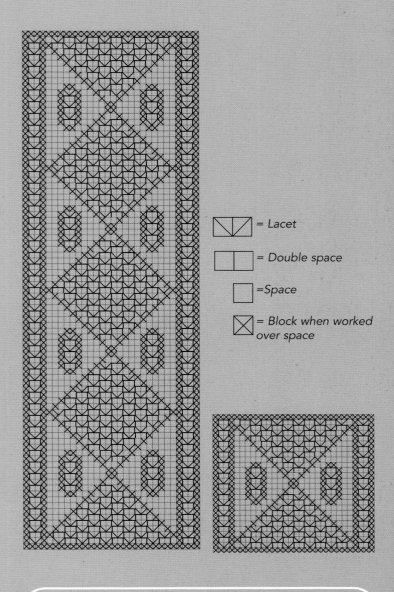

= Lacet

= Double space

=Space

= Block when worked over space

THIS PROJECT WAS CREATED WITH 2 skeins of Red Heart's *Baby Sport Pompadour* in White (#1001), 90% acrylic/10% olefin, 6oz/170g = 480yd/439m

SKILL LEVEL: INTERMEDIATE

Finished Measurements
One size fits most
Neck edge: 32"/81cm
circumference
Bottom edge: 88"/224cm
circumference
Length: 26"/66cm from V at
neck edge to point at center
front

YOU WILL NEED
Approx 560 yd/512m
worsted weight ribbbon yarn
(A)
Approx 55yd/50m eyelash
railroad yarn (B)
Hook: 6.50mm/K–10½ or size
needed to obtain gauge

STITCHES USED
Chain stitch (ch)
Double crochet (dc)
Double treble crochet (dtr)
Single crochet (sc)
Slip stitch (sl st)

SPECIAL STITCH TECHNIQUE
V-stitch (V-st): Dtr, ch 2, dtr
in same st or sp

GAUGE
*Take time to check
your gauge.*
With A, 13 sts and 4 rows in
pattern = 4"/10cm

LACY RIBBON PONCHO • *Designed by Kalpna Kapoor*

The open-mesh pattern of this poncho lends itself nicely to those luscious (and fun to work with) ribbon yarns.

Pattern

Starting at neck edge, with one strand each of A and B held tog as one, ch 104, and without twisting ch, close into a ring with 1 sl st in first ch. Drop B, continue with A only.

Rnd 1: Ch 7 (counts as dc, ch 4), skip next 3 ch, *dc in next ch, ch 4, skip next 3 ch; rep from * around. Sl st in 3rd ch of turning ch to join (26 ch-4 sps).

Rnd 2: Sl st in first ch-4 sp, ch 7 (counts as dtr, ch 2), dtr in first st, ch 2, (V-st, ch 2) in each ch-4 sp around. Sl st to 5th ch of turning ch to join (26 V-sts).

Rnd 3: Ch 7(counts as dc, ch 4), dc in same st (inc made), *ch 4, skip next V-st, dc in next ch-2 sp*; rep from * to * 11 times, skip next V-st, (dc, ch 4, dc) in next ch-2 sp (inc made), rep from * to * 12 times. Sl st in 3rd ch of turning ch to join (28 ch-4 sps). Place a marker in each inc sp, move marker up as work progresses.

Rnd 4: Sl st in first ch-4 sp, ch 5 (counts as dtr), (ch 2, dtr, ch-2, V-st) in the same st (inc made), ch-2, (V-st, ch 2) in each ch-4 sp around, working (V-st, ch 2, V-st, ch 2) in next marked sp (inc made). Sl st to 5th ch of turning ch to join (30 V-sts).

Rnds 5–20: Rep Rnds 3-4 for pattern, inc 2 V-sts in every other rnd on each side (64 V-sts in last rnd). Fasten off A.

Bottom Edging With RS facing, join 2 strands of B in any dtr on bottom edge, ch 1, *sc in dtr, sc in next ch-2 sp; rep from * around. Sl st in first sc to join (128 sc). Fasten off.

Neck Edging With RS facing, working across opposite side of foundation, join 2 strands of B in any ch-3 sp on neck edge, ch 1, work 3 sc in each ch-3 sp around. Sl st in first sc to join (78 sc). Fasten off.

THIS PROJECT WAS CREATED WITH 7 balls of Crystal Palace Deco-Ribbon in #9399, 70 % acrylic/30% nylon, 1¾oz/50g = 80yd/73m

1 ball of Trendsetter Crisantemo in black (#2) 80% polyester/15% viscose, 1¾oz/50g = 55yd/50m

poncho is obtained by introducing a new color in each row. Alternate light and dark colors. Variegated yarns can be worked for several rows, giving the effect of a new color in each row. Solids and heathers should be changed at the end of each row.

Try a new color for a few stitches. If you don't like the effect, take out the stitches and try another color. It is sometimes helpful to lay out a number of rows of colors using the skeins of yarn to get an idea of how they will look when crocheted.

PONCHO FRAMED • *Designed by Linda Buckner*

SKILL LEVEL: INTERMEDIATE

FINISHED MEASUREMENTS
One size fits most.
49"/125cm wide x
27"/69cm long

YOU WILL NEED
Approx 2000yd/1828m of worsted yarns*
Approx 132yd/121m of bulky tufted yarn (A)
Hook: 8mm/L-11or size needed to obtain gauge
* Select a variety of worsted weight solid, heather, and variegated yarns in your choice of color and fiber content. Use as many or as few colors as desired.

STITCHES USED
Chain stitch (ch)
Double crochet (dc)
Half double crochet (hdc)
Slip stitch (sl st)

SPECIAL STITCH TECHNIQUES
Front post double crochet (fpdc): Yo, insert hook from front to back to front again, around the post of designated st, yo, draw yarn through st and up to level of current row, (yo, draw yarn through 2 loops on hook) twice.
Back post double crochet (bpdc): Yo, insert hook from back to front to back again, around the post of designated st, yo, draw yarn through st and up to level of current row, (yo, draw yarn through 2 loops on hook) twice.

GAUGE
Take time to check your gauge.
9 sts and 8 rows in post st pattern = 4"/10cm

PATTERN NOTES
While this poncho is reversible, for the ease of working, the front post double crochet side is designated as the right side and the the back post double crochet is the wrong side. The ch-3 turning ch counts as a stitch throughout. The graphic impact of this

Words like graphic and bold describe this poncho. Simple striping combined with a strong color palette makes it a fun, one-of-a-kind fashion statement.

Front/Back Triangle (make 2)

Starting at center top edge, with desired color, ch 3 and close into a ring with 1 sl st in first ch.

Row 1 (RS): Ch 3, 2 dc in ring, (ch 1, 3 dc) twice in ring, turn.

Row 2: Ch 3, dc in first st (inc made), fpdc around the post of each of next 2 dc, dc in next ch-1 sp, fpdc around the post of next dc, 3 dc in next dc (center point), fpdc around the post of next dc, dc in next ch-1 sp, fpdc around the post of each of next 2 dc, 2 dc in top of turning ch (inc made), turn.

Row 3: Ch 3, bpdc around the post of each st across to center dc, 3 dc in next dc (center point), bpdc around the post of each of st across, turn.

Row 4: Ch 3, dc in first st (inc made), fpdc around the post of each st across to center dc at point, 3 dc in next dc (center point), fpdc around the post of each st across to last st, 2 dc in top of turning ch (inc made), turn.

Rep Rows 3–4 until triangle measures desired width and length. (The poncho pictured is worked with 37 rows or until it measures 46"/117cm wide x 28"/71cm long.)

Neckline

Row 1 (RS): When the desired width and length of each side is completed, with desired color, ch 3, working around the tops of sts whenever possible, work approximately 3 sts for every 2 rows, fpdc evenly across top edge top top left-hand corner st, turn (106 sts). Continue to change color at end of each row as before.

Row 2: Ch 3, dc in first st, fpdc around the post of each st across, turn (106 sts).

First Shoulder Inset

Row 3: Mark the center 22 sts (for 10"/25cm neck opening), ch 3, fpdc around the post of each st across to first marker.

Row 4: Ch 3, fpdc around the post of each st across, turn.

Row 5: With the same color as Row 4, ch 3, bpdc around the post of each st across, turn.

Rows 6–7: Rep Rows 4–5. Fasten off.

Second Shoulder Inset

Row 3: With RS facing, skip center 22 sts, join same color as Row 3 of First shoulder inset in next st, ch 3, fpdc around the post of each st across, turn.

Rep Neckline and Shoulder Insets on other triangle.

Finishing

With right sides facing, sew or slip stitch triangles together across shoulder insets.

Neck Border

Rnd 1: With RS facing, attach your choice of color to 1 shoulder seam, ch 3, dc around neckline. Sl st in 3rd ch of turning ch to join. Fasten off.

Rnd 2 (RS): Attach A in front loop of any st in Rnd 1, ch 2, hdc in front loop only of each st around. Sl st in 2nd ch of turning ch to join, turn. Fasten off.

Rnd 3: With WS facing, with A, ch 2, working in rem loops in Rnd 1, hdc in rem front loop of each st around. Sl st in 2nd ch of turning ch to join. Fasten off.

Bottom Border

Rnd 1: With RS facing, attach A around the post of any st on bottom edge of Poncho, ch 2, hdc in front loop only of each st around bottom edge, working 3 hdc in center st at each bottom point. Sl st in 2nd ch of turning ch to join.

Rnd 2: With RS facing, ch 3, working in rem loops of sts in last row of poncho, dc in back loop only of each st around bottom edge, working 3 hdc in center st at each bottom point. Sl st in 3rd ch of turning ch to join. Fasten off.

THIS PROJECT WAS CREATED WITH 1 skein each of Noro's *Kureyon* in #52 and #147, 100% wool, 1¾ oz/50g = 109yd/100m

2 skeins each of Noro's *Kureyon* in #92, #138, #88, #124, and #126, 100% wool, 1 3/4oz/50g = 109yd/100m

1 skein of Manos del Uruguay in #51, 100% wool, 138 yd/126m

1 skein of Mountain Colors' 3 ply *Montana Wool* in Alpine , 100% wool, 4oz/112g = 150yd/137m.

1 skein of Classic Elite's *Montera* in various colors, 50% Llama/50% wool, 3½oz/100g = 128yd/116m

1 ball of Tahki's *Soho Bulky Tweed* (#395), 100% wool, 3½oz/100g = 110yd/99m

4 skeins of Gedifra *Sheela* in black (#4114), 48% wool/48% acrylic/4% nylon, 1 3/4oz/50g = 33yd/30m

HEXAGON PONCHO • *Designed by Linda Buckner*

SKILL LEVEL: INTERMEDIATE

FINISHED MEASUREMENTS
One size fits most
Poncho: 43"/109cm wide x 32"/81cm long
Hat: 21"/53cm in circumference

YOU WILL NEED
Approx 3000yd/2743m yarn*
Hook: 7mm/K-10½ or size needed to obtain gauge
Yarn needle

*A variety of worsted and bulky weight yarns (mohairs, bouclés, slubs, ribbon, chenilles, smooth, eyelash and novelty yarns), composed of manmade and natural fibers in the same color family. The designer used approximately 35 skeins in 21 shades of red, burgundy, purple, and anything in between. Use as many or as few colors as desired.

Oh, go ahead. Gather up and group all those stashed yarns into color families and crochet this wonderful assemblage of hexagons. Better yet, go out and buy a whole new stash of yarns! Set your creative shopping-self free.

> *Loop stitch (loop st):* Place 4 fingers of left hand over st to be worked, wrap yarn from front to back around 4 fingers forming a 3"/8cm loop, insert hook in next st, yo, draw yarn through st, yo, draw yarn through 2 loops on hook.
>
> The reverse side of front post double crochet is a back post double crochet. Either side of a hexagon can be designated as the the right side.
>
> A 3"/8cm piece of cardboard may be used in place of your fingers, to wrap yarn around when working a loop stitch.

Hexagon Motif (make 52)

Ch 4 and close into a ring with 1 sl st in first ch.

Rnd 1: Ch 3, dc in ring, ch 1 (2 dc, ch 1) 5 times in ring. Sl st in 3rd ch of turning ch to join (6 ch-1 sps).

Rnd 2: Ch 4 (counts as one dc, ch 1), *fpdc around the post of each of next 2 dc**, (dc, ch 1, dc) in next ch-1 sp; rep from * around, ending at **. Sl st in 3rd ch of turning ch to join (6 ch-1 sps).

Rnd 3: Sl st to first ch-1 sp, ch 4, dc in same ch-1 space, *fpdc around the post of each of next 4 dc**, (dc, ch 1, dc) in next ch-1 sp; rep from * around, ending with **. Sl st in 3rd ch of turning ch to join (6 ch-1 sps).

Rnd 4: Rep Rnd 3 (6 ch-1 sps; 6 groups of 8 dc on each side). Fasten off.

Assembly

Use either side of the hexagons as desired for the right side of the poncho.

Arrange hexagons following diagram (figure 1)

Use a yarn needle and desired color of yarn to sew hexagons together or use a K–10 ½ crochet hook to crochet hexagons together. Work a single crochet in each double crochet and each corner chain-1 space across each side.

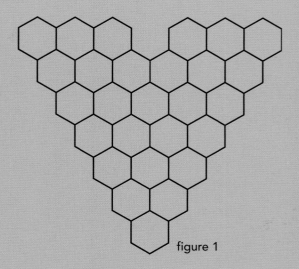

figure 1

Bottom Edging

Rnd 1: With chosen RS of poncho facing, join choice of yarn in bottom corner ch-1 sp on lowest hexagon of back, ch 4, dc in same ch-1 sp, working in same st as the hexagon you are working in, fpdc (or bpdc) in each st across to next ch-1 sp, (dc, ch 1, dc) in next ch-1 sp, continue to work around in pattern established by hexagon motifs, work fpdc or bpdc in pattern around the seam stitch. Sl st in 3rd ch of turning ch to join. Fasten off.

Rnd 2: With RS of poncho facing, join choice of yarn in bottom ch-1 sp in lowest hexagon on front, rep Rnd 1, working dc2tog in pattern at each junction between hexagons. Sl st in 3rd ch of turning ch to join. Fasten off.

Rnd 3: With RS of poncho facing, join choice of yarn in first ch-1 sp, ch 1, (sc, ch 1, sc) in ch-1 space, sc in each st around, working (sc, ch 1, sc) in each ch-1 space, and working sc2tog at each junction between Hexagons. Sl st in first sc to join. Fasten off.

Neckline Edging

Rnd 1: With RS facing, join choice of yarn in any dc on neck edge, ch 2, sc in each st around, working a sc before and after the seam. Sl st in 2nd ch of turning ch to join.

Rnd 2: With RS facing, using an eyelash or feathery yarn, and working inside the neck opening, join yarn in back loop of any st, ch 2, loop st in back loop of each st around. Sl st in 2nd ch of turning ch to join, turn.

Rnd 3: With WS facing, ch 2, loop st in back loop of each st in Rnd 1 around. Sl st in 2nd ch of turning ch to join. Fasten off. Weave in ends.

Beret

Hexagon motifs (make 5)

Ch 4 and close into a ring with 1 sl st in first ch.

Rnd 1: Ch 3, dc in ring, ch 1 (2 dc, ch 1) 5 times in ring. Sl st in 3rd ch of turning ch to join (6 ch-1 sps).

Rnd 2: Ch 4 (counts as one dc, ch 1), *fpdc around the post of each of next 2 dc**, (dc, ch 1, dc) in next ch-1 sp; rep from * around, ending at **. Sl st in 3rd ch of turning ch to join (6 ch-1 sps).

Rnd 3: Sl st to first ch-1 sp, ch 4, dc in same ch-1 space, *fpdc around the post of each of next 4 dc**, (dc, ch 1, dc) in next ch-1 sp; rep from * around, ending with **. Sl st in 3rd ch of turning ch to join (6 ch-1 sps).

Rnd 4: Rep Rnd 3 (6 ch-1 sps; 6 groups of 8 dc on each side). Fasten off.

Pentagon Motif (make 1)

Ch 4 and close into a ring with 1 sl st in first ch.

Rnd 1: Ch 3, dc in ring, ch 1 (2 dc, ch 1) 4 times in ring. Sl st in 3rd ch of turning ch to join (5 ch-1 sps).

Rnd 2: Ch 4 (counts as one dc, ch 1), *fpdc around the post of each of next 2 dc**, (dc, ch 1, dc) in next ch-1 space; rep from * around, ending at **. Sl st in 3rd ch of turning ch to join (5 ch-1 sps).

Rnd 3: Sl st to first ch-1 sp, ch 4, dc in same ch-1 space, *fpdc around the post of each of next 4 dc**, (dc, ch 1, dc) in next ch-1 sp; rep from * around, ending with **. Sl st in 3rd ch of turning ch to join (5 ch-1 sps).

Rnd 4: Rep Rnd 3. (5 ch-1 sps; 5 groups of 8 dc on each side). Fasten off.

Assembly

Sew or use a K–10 ½ hook to single crochet the 5 hexagons together (figure 2). Sew or crochet the pentagon (easing to fit) to the inner edges of the hexagons. Sew or single crochet the open side seams of the hexagons.

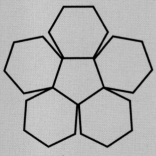

figure 2

Edging

Rnd 1: With RS facing, join chosen color in any sc on bottom edge of hat, ch 2, sc in each st and space around bottom edge of hat. Sl st in 2nd ch of turning ch to join, turn. Fasten off.

Rnd 2: With WS facing, join chosen color in any sc, ch 2 and place marker, *sl st in next st, hdc in next st; rep from * around, do not join, work in a spiral.

Rnd 3: Rep Rnd 2, ending with a sl st in marked st. Fasten off.

Note: If you need a larger size, place hat over a form (a bowl will work) of the size you need. Spritz with water, and let dry.

THIS PROJECT WAS CREATED WITH 1 skein each of Mountain Colors *Mohair* in Flathead Cherry and Ruby River, 78% mohair/13% wool/9% nylon, 3 1/2oz/100g = 225yd/206m.

1 skein each of Mountain Colors *Moguls* in Flathead Cherry and Ruby River, 98% wool/ 2% nylon, 65yd/59m.

1 skein each of Mountain Colors *Merino Ribbon* in Flathead Cherry and Ruby River, 80% super fine merino wool/20% nylon, 245yd/224m

1 skein each of Mountain Colors *Wooly Feathers* in Flathead Cherry and Ruby River, 65% kid mohair/35% nylon/85yd/78m

5 skeins of Mountain Colors *Noro Kureyon* in Burgundy #124, 100% wool, 110yd/101m

1 skein Muench *Touch Me* in bright red (#3600); 3 balls in purple (#3601); 3 skeins in burgundy (#3620), 72% viscose microfiber/28% new wool, 61yd/56m

1 skein of Filatura Di Crosa *Tokyo* in #13, 55% extra fine Merino wool/35% polyester/10% polyamid, 71yd/65m

2 skeins of Trendsetter Checkmate in #F1010, 100% nylon, 70yd/64m

2 skeins of Berroco *Opulent FX* in #7822, 100% nylon, 103yd/94m

5 skeins of Debbie Bliss *Alpaca Silk* in burgundy (#25011), 80% baby alpaca/ 20% silk, 1 ¾oz/50g = 71yd/65m

3 skeins of Muench *Cleo* in #132 and 1 skein in #122, 87% viscose/13% metal, 1 3/4oz/50g = 62yd/57m

1 skein of Plymouth Yarn *Frizzato* in #1115, 87% nylon/13% rayon, 1 3/4oz/50g = 77yd/70m

1 skein each of Manos del Uruguay in #57 and #66, 100% kettle-dyed wool, 3 1/2oz/100g = 135yd/122m

SKILL LEVEL: INTERMEDIATE

FINISHED MEASUREMENTS
One size fits most
Wrap: 41"/104cm long x
14"/36cm (before assembly)

YOU WILL NEED
165yd/151m worsted
weight mohair/wool blend
yarn in onyx (A) and pink (B)
330yd/302m sport weight
ribbon yarn in multicolor
(C); and 165yd/151m in
black (D)
124yd/113m worsted
weight angora/wool
blend yarn in black (E)
and pink (F).
Optional for Floral embellishments:
61yd/56m worsted weight
chenille yarn in black (G)
and olive (H)

Hook for body: size
9mm/M–13 or size needed
to obtain gauge
Hook for trim: size
6mm/L–11 or size needed
to obtain gauge
Hook for cloche: size
5.5mm/I–9 or size needed
to obtain gauge
Hook for floral embellishments: size 3.5mm/E or
size needed to obtain
gauge, for flowers and
leaves

STITCHES USED
Chain stitch (ch)
Double crochet (dc)
Single crochet (sc)
Triple crochet (tr)

SPECIAL STITCH PATTERN
Knot stitch (knot st): *Draw
up a loop on hook to

Don't wear this romantic wisp of a poncho if it's warmth that you seek. Unless, of course, you're planning to heat up the room with your presence. In that case, you're all set!

Wrap

With M-13 hook and 1 strand each of B and C held tog, ch 92.

Row 1: *Work 2 knot sts, skip the first 3 ch, sc in the next ch; rep from * across to last, turn (23 double loops).

Row 2: Work 2 knot sts, *sc in center of next 2 knot sts, work 2 knot sts; * repeat from * to * across, sc in center of last 2 knot sts, turn (23 double loops). Fasten off B, join A.

Rep Row 2 until Wrap measures 14"/36cm from beg, working in the following color sequence: *2 rows with A and C held together as one; 2 rows with B and C held together as one; rep from * throughout. Fasten off.

Assembly

Mark corners A, B, and C as shown in figure 1 (with the beginning chain side B to C). Mark position D, 15"/38cm up from edge as shown. Pin corner B to

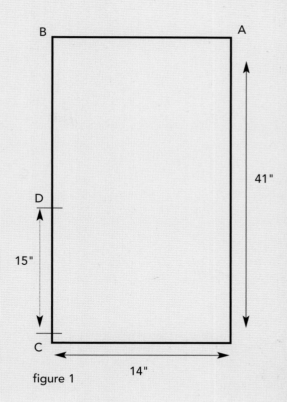

figure 1

marked position D, and then pin corner A to corner C. With yarn needle and B yarn, sew seam from A/C to B/D. (The beginning chain should form the neck opening).

ROMANTIC LITTLE WRAP & CLOCHE • *Designed by Linda Buckne*

1"/25mm, yo, draw yarn through long loop on hook, insert hook in single strand (bottom part) of long loop just made, yo, draw yarn through loop, yo, draw yarn through 2 loops on hook (1 knot st complete); rep from * once (double loop complete).

GAUGE
Take time to check your gauge.
Wrap and hat: (Sc, 2 knot sts) twice and 3 rows in pattern = 4"/10cm
Brim pattern: 12 sts = 4"/10cm

PATTERN NOTES
Beginning chain counts as a stitch throughout.
With M-13 hook and 1 strand each of B and C held tog, work two pattern rows, change to onyx and one strand multicolor held together, work two pattern rows, alternating colors in this manner until piece measures 14"/35.6 cm in width.

Bottom Edging

Rows 1–2: With B and C held tog, join yarn at front point. Work in established pattern of double loops around bottom edge. Sl st in base of first knot st to join.

Row 3: With L-11 hook and 1 strand each of F and D held together as one, ch 2, 2 sc in the same space, *ch 4, sc in center of next 2 knot sts, rep from * around. Sl st in 2nd ch of turning ch to join. Fasten off B, join D.

Row 4: With C and D held tog, ch 2, sc in each st around. Sl st in 2nd ch of turning ch to join. Fasten off C and D, join 1 strand of E.

Row 5: With E, ch 2, sc in each st around. Sl st in 2nd ch of turning ch to join.

Rnd 6: Work 2 knot sts, skip 1 sc, sc in the next sc, *work 2 knot sts, skip 3 sc, sc in the next sc*; rep from * around to last work 1 knot st. Sl st in 1st knot st to join. Fasten off.

Neck Edging

Row 1: With RS facing, using M-13 hook, join 1 strand of F in any st on neck opening, ch 2, sc in each ch and each sc around. Sl st in 2nd ch of turning ch to join. Fasten off F.

Row 2: With RS facing, join 1 strand each of C and D, ch 2, sc in each ch and each sc around, working 3 incs evenly spaced around. Sl st in 2nd ch of turning ch to join. Fasten off C and D

Row 3: With RS facing, join 1 strand of D in any sc, ch 1, *hdc in next st, sl st in next st; rep from * around. Sl st in ch-1 turning ch to join. Fasten off.

Fringe

Cut 12"/30cm lengths of A and B for fringe. Using 1 strand each of A and B for each fringe, attach one doubled length in the center of each double loop around bottom edge of the wrap.

Large Flower (optional)

With E-4 hook and G, ch 6 and close into a ring with 1 sl st in first ch.

Rnd 1: Ch 1, (sc, ch 5) 8 times in ring. Sl st in first sc to join (8 ch-5 loops).

Rnd 2: Sl st in 1st ch-5 loop, ch 1, (sc, ch 1, [dc, ch 1] 5 times, sc) in each ch-5 loop around. Sl st in first sc to join (8 petals). Fasten off.

Small Flower

With E-4 hook and B, ch 5 and close into a ring with 1 sl st in first ch.

Rnd 1: (Ch 4, 2 tr, ch 4, sl st) 5 times in ring. Fasten off.

Flower Center

With C, wrap around 2 fingers about 10x's, cut yarn. With a small length of multicolor yarn, tie securely through the center of wound circle, cut strands to make a tassel.

Assemble flower

Sew small flower to center of large flower. Tie the tassel in the center of both flowers.

Leaves

With E-4 hook and H, ch 15.

Sl st in 2nd ch from hook, sc in each of next 2 ch, hdc in each of next 2 ch, dc in each of next 2 ch, tr in each of next 2 ch, ch 4, sl st in ch at base of same tr, skip last 5 ch, working across opposite side of foundation ch, sl st in same ch at base of last tr, ch 4, tr in same ch, tr in next ch, dc in each of next 2 ch, hdc in each of next 2 ch, sc in each of next 2 ch, sl st in next ch, ch 3, sl st in 3rd ch from hook (picot), sl st in next sl st, sl st in each of next 8 sts, sl st in each ch of ch-4 loop, sl st in ch at base of ch-4 loop, sl st in next ch of foundation ch, ch 4, tr in same ch, dc in next ch, hdc in next ch, sc in next ch, sl st in next ch, ch 3, sl st in 3rd ch from hook, working across opposite side of foundation ch, sl st in next ch, sc in next ch, hdc in next ch, dc in next ch, tr in next ch, ch 4, sl st in same ch as last tr made. Fasten off.

Place assembled flower on top of leaves. Sew the leaves and flowers to the V of the neck edge.

Cloche

Use I-9 hook and 1 strand ea of B and C held tog, ch 5 and close into a ring with 1 sl st in first ch.

Rnd 1: Ch 3, work 1 knot st, (dc, 1 knot st) 8 times in ring. Sl st in 3rd ch of turning ch to join (9 knot sts).

Rnd 2: Ch 3, work 1 knot st, dc in top of turning ch, *work 1 knot st, (dc, knot st, dc) in next dc; rep from * around, ending with 1 knot st. Sl st in 3rd ch of turning ch to join (18 knot sts).

Rnds 3–6: *Work 2 knot sts, skip next 2 knot sts, sc in next dc; rep from * around, ending with 1 knot st, dc in base of first knot st to join (9 double loops).

Rnd 7: *Work 2 knot sts, skip next 2 knot sts, sc in next dc; rep from * around, ending with 2 knot sts, sl st in base of first knot st to join (9 double loops).

Rnd 8: *Ch 6 (for larger size, ch 7), skip double knot st, sc in next sc; rep from * around. Sl st in base of first ch-5 loop to join (9 ch-6 [ch-7] loops). Fasten off B.

Hat Brim

This pattern stitch is produced on the wrong side.

Rnd 1: With WS facing, join A in first sc, ch 2, mark beginning of round, *sl st in next st, hdc in next st; rep from * around, do not join, work in a spiral (63 [72] sts). Mark beg of rnd and move marker up as work progresses.

Rnd 2: Rep Rnd 1.

Rnd 3: *Sl st in next st, hdc in next st, sl st in next st, 2 hdc in next st (inc made); rep from * around (54 [63] sts).

Rep Rnd 3 until brim measures 1½"/4cm from beg.

Add 1 strand of C, with 1 strand each of A and C, rep Rnd 3 for 2 more rnds. Fasten off A and C.

Finishing

If desired, make a small and large flower with leaves (as above) to embellish the cloche.

Fold one side of brim up and tack in place.

Sew flowers and leaves to unfolded brim edge of cloche.

THIS PROJECT WAS CREATED WITH 1 skein each of Fiesta Yarns' *LaBoheme* in onyx and abalone, 64% brushed kid mohair/28% wool/8% nylon and 100% rayon boucle, 4oz/112g = 145 yd/130m

2 balls of Plymouth Yarn's *Eros* in multi (#1119), 100% nylon, 1¾oz/50g = 165 yd/151m

1 ball of Plymouth Yarn's *Eros* in black (#3017), 100% nylon, 1¾oz/50g = 165 yd/151m

1 skein each of Classic Elite *Lush* in Black (#4413) and Pink Icing (#4419), 50% angora/50% wool, 1¾oz/50g = 123yd/111m

Flowers

1 ball each of Muench Yarns' *Touch Me* in black (#3607) and olive green (#3610), 72% rayon microfibers/ 28% new wool, 1¾oz/50g = 61yd/56m

A lacey wisp of a poncho is created with unusual stitch techniques showcasing the delicate colors, airy textures, and just a hint of metallic sheen.

ble-ended hook. Place a point protector on the end to keep stitches from coming off.

To work the OLO Loop Row, ch 2, skip 1st esc (Note: loop on the hook counts as the 1st OLO loop), *insert hook in next esc, yo, draw yarn through st and draw up to level of work (approximately 1"/2.5cm); rep from * across row to last st, Insert hook into last stitch, and draw up a loop to level of work, yo, draw yarn through st, yo, draw through all loops on hook. Ending ch counts as 1 st.

GAUGE
Take time to check your gauge.
Using J-10 double-ended flexi hook, with 1 strand each of A and B held together as one, 9 sts = 4"/10cm; 4 rows in pattern = 2½"/6cm
Using I-9 hook and C, 10 sts = 4"/10cm

PATTERN NOTES
If you'd like to make another size or use a different weight of yarn, begin with a chain which is divisible by 6.

CHANTEL • *Designed by Joan A. Davis*

SKILL LEVEL: EXPERIENCED

FINISHED MEASUREMENTS
Women's sizes S (M,L)
Neck edge: 34 (38, 41)"/86 (96, 104)cm
Bottom edge: 92 (104, 113)"/234 (264, 287)cm
Length: 13½"/34cm

YOU WILL NEED
550 (660, 770)yd/503 (604, 704)m worsted weight novelty yarn (A)
570 (684, 798)yd/521 (625, 730)m sport weight novelty yarn (B)
260yd (520, 520)yd/238 (475, 475)m DK weight natural fiber yarn (C)
Hooks: size 5.5mm/I-9 and 6mm/J–10 circular double-ended hook, 40"/102cm long or size needed for gauge.*
25 stitch markers
Shoulder pads (optional)
*You can substitute a 6mm/J–10 Flexi Afghan hook and a 6mm/J–10 standard hook if desired.

STITCHES USED
Chain stitch (ch)
Single crochet (sc)
Extended single crochet (esc)

Special Stitch Techniques
Extended single crochet decrease (esc2tog): (Insert hook in next st, yo, draw yarn through st) twice, yo draw yarn through 3 loops on hook.
Omega Lace crochet is worked on 2 rows.
Omega Lace Off row (OLF): Esc is the OLF row. The OLF row anchors the loops.
To work the OLF row, ch 1, *insert hook into next st, yo, draw yarn through st (2 loops on hook), yo, draw yarn through 1 loop on hook st (2 loops on hook), yo, draw yarn through 2 loops on hook, remove loop from double-ended hook; rep from * across.
Omega Loop On Row (OLO): Loop is the second part of the stitch called OLO or Omega Loop On row. This part of the stitch is worked on the flexi dou-

Pattern

Starting at neck edge, with 5.5mm/I-9 standard hook, and 1 strand each of A and B held tog as one, ch 108 (120, 132).

Row 1 (RS): Sc in 2nd ch from hook, sc in each sc across, turn (107 [119, 131] sc).

Row 2 (inc row): Ch 1, *esc in each of next 5 sc, 2 esc in next sc; rep from * across, ending with esc in each of last 5 sc, turn (123 [138, 152] esc).

Row 3 OLO: With J-10 double-ended hook, ch 2, work OLO in each st across row to last st, in last st, work ending ch, turn (123 [138, 152] loops on hook).

Row OLF: With I-9 standard hook, insert hook in first loop on double-ended hook, yo, draw yarn through lp, esc in same lp, remove lp from double-ended hook, esc in next lp on double-ended hook, remove lp from hook; rep from * across, turn (123 [138, 152] esc).

Row 5 OLO (inc row): With J-10 double-ended hook, ch 2, work OLO in each of next 4 esc, 2 OLO in next esc, *work OLO in each of next 5 esc, 2 OLO in next esc; * rep from * across to last 3 (0, 2), OLO in each of last 3 (0, 2) esc, turn (143 [161, 175] lps on hook).

Row 6 (OLF): ch 1, esc in each st around, sl st in first esc in Row 6 to join, do not turn (143 [161, 175] esc), Work now progresses in rnds.

Rnd 7 OLO (inc row): With J-10 double-ended hook, ch 2, work OLO in each of next 4 esc, 2 OLO in next esc, *work OLO in each of next 5 esc, 2 OLO in next esc; * rep from * across to last 5 (5, 1) sts, OLO in each of last 5 (5, 1) sts, sl st in first loop on hook to join (166 [187, 204] loops).

Rnd 8 OLF: With I-9 standard hook, ch 1, esc in each st around, sl st in first esc to join (166 [187, 204] esc).

Rnd 9 OLO (inc row): With J-10 double-ended hook, ch 2, work OLO in next 2 esc, 2 OLO in next esc, *work OLO in each of next 3 esc, 2 OLO in next esc; * rep from * across to last 2 (3, 0) esc, OLO in each of last 2 (3, 0) esc, turn (207 [233, 255] lps on hook).

Rnd 10 OLF: Rep Row 8 (207 [233, 255] esc).

Rnd 11 OLF: With J-10 double-ended hook, ch 2, work OLO in each esc around, sl st in first lp on hook to join (207 [233, 255] lps on hook).

Rnds 12–35: Rep Rnds 10–11. If a longer poncho is desired, continue to work even until desired length is achieved. Fasten off A and B.

Rnd 36: With RS facing, using I-9 standard hook, attach C in first loop, ch 1, esc in each st around, sl st in first esc to join. Fasten off C. Weave in ends.

Neck Edging

Row 1: With I-9 standard hook, working across opposite side of foundation ch, join C in 1st ch, work esc in each esc across, turn (107 [119, 131] sc).

Row 2 (dec row): Ch 1, *esc in each of next 3 esc, sc2tog in next 2 sts; rep from * across, ending with esc in last 2 (4, 1) esc, turn (86 [96, 105] esc).

Row 3: Ch 10 (button loop), esc in each esc across, working 1 (2, 2) dec evenly spaced across, turn (85 [94, 103] esc).

Row 4: Ch 1, esc in 1st esc, *skip next 2 sts, (2 dc, ch 3, sc) in next st; rep from * across, ending with esc in last esc (27 [30, 33] shells).

Button (make 2)

With I-9 standard hook and C, ch 6 and close into a ring with 1 sl st in first ch.

Rnd 1: Insert hook in ring, yo, draw yarn through ring, yo, draw yarn through loop on hook and up to ½"/13mm, drop loop from hook; rep from * 15 times in ring, insert hook in ring, draw yarn through ring, ch 10. Fasten off, leaving a sewing length. Sew end of ch-10 on both buttons to top corner of neck edging opposite button loop.

THIS PROJECT WAS CREATED WITH A: 10(12,14) skeins of Berroco *Lavish* in Donatella (#7319), 1¾oz/50g = 55yd/50m

B: 10(12,14) skeins of Berroco *Jewel FX* in Alexandrites (#6910), 7/8oz/25g = 57yd/52m

C: 2(4) skeins of Berroco *Pleasure* in Soft Blue (#8614), 1¾oz/50g = 130yd/120m

SKILL LEVEL: EXPERIENCED

FINISHED MEASUREMENTS
One size fits most
Width: 120"/305cm in circumference
Length: 28"/71cm

YOU WILL NEED
Approx 1760yd/1609m worsted
weight yarn
Hooks: sizes 7mm/K–10½ and
8mm/L–11 afghan or cro-hook or size
needed to obtain gauge
Yarn needle
U-shaped cable needle (optional)

STITCHES USED
Chain stitch (ch)
Tunisian Simple Stitch (Tss)*
Tunisian Purl Stitch (Tps)*
Tunisian Knit Stitch (Tks)*
*See page 000

SPECIAL TERMS AND STITCHES
Forward Row (F Row): First half of a
Tunisian row, worked from right to left.
Return Row (R Row): Second half of a
Tunisian row, worked from left to right.
Edge Stitch (edge st): Always work the
last st of each row as Tss, inserting
hook under the final vertical thread
plus the one just behind it before
pulling through a loop. The loop on
the hook before beginning a Forward

(cont'd on page 94)

ASHLEY TUNISIAN PONCHO •

Designed by Kathleen Power Johnson
Crocheted by Katherine Mancinho

This is a great project for the experienced crocheter who wishes to expand her (or his!) repertoire. Tunisian crochet is not difficult to master, and the addition of special stitches makes this garment a showstopper.

Row is the right edge stitch and counts as the 1st stitch of the row.

Working Stitch (working st): The 1st loop on the hook after a yo is pulled through 2 loops.

Right Cross (RC): On R Row, work up the Tks to be crossed to the right, drop the working st and the next st (a Tks) from hook and hold the Tks lp on a cable needle to the front of work. Replace working st on hook, yo, draw through 2 lps on hook, drop working st from hook and insert hook in held st. Then working lp, yo, draw through 2 lps on hook. On the next F Row, work stitches in new order.

Left Cross (LC): On R Row, work up to 1 st before the next Tks (not counting the working st on the hook), drop the working st and the next st (a Tps) from hook, and hold the Tps loop on a cable needle to the back of work. Replace working st on hook, yo, draw through 2 lps on hook, drop working st from hook and insert hook in held st; then working lp, yo, draw through 2 lps on hook. On the next F Row, work stitches in new order.

Cable on R Row: Work off the designated number of sts, drop 1st (working) st

from hook, place the next st, a Tks, on cable needle and hold to the front of work. Replace working stitch on hook, work off next Tks, drop working st from hook, transfer st from cable needle to hook, then replace working st, and work off sts as usual.

GAUGE
Take time to check your gauge.

13 sts and 11 rows = 4"/10cm in Tunisian Purl Stitch (tps) using size L-11 afghan hook

PATTERN NOTES
One Forward (F Row) and Return (R Row) equals one row of Tunisian Crochet. It is assumed that the R Row is always worked the same way and the instructions for the R Row are omitted except for those on which a cross or cable occur.

The first stitch is always worked into the second vertical thread from the edge.

The first and second to last stitches are always worked as Tks.

Bind off: At the beginning of the row, form stitch as usual for current row, finish the row with a slip stitched edge.

Increase (Inc): On an F Row, insert hook into bump behind a stitch and pull through a loop.

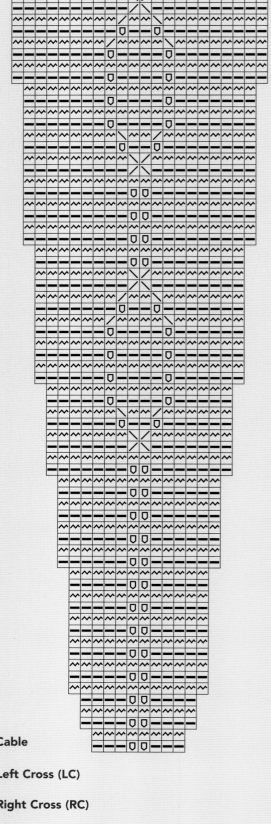

 Cable

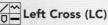 **Left Cross (LC)**

Right Cross (RC)

Tunisian Knit Stitch (TKs)

Tunisian Purl Stitch (Tps)

Return row

Panel (Make 4)

Ch 19.

F Row 1: Working into the single thread beneath the ch, pull up a loop in the 2nd ch from hook and in each ch across (18 loops). Work R Row, and cont to work R Row after each F Row throughout.

F Row 2: Tks, (2 Tps, 2 Tks) 3 times, 2 Tps, Tks, edge st (18 loops)

F Row 3: Tks, inc, (2 Tps, inc, 2 Tks, inc) 3 times, 2 Tps, inc, Tks, edge st (26 loops).

F Rows 4–72: Work in patt as established following chart, repeating Rows 10–21 for pattern. On Rows 2, 4, 8, 12, 18, 24, 31, 44, 56, and 70 work incs after 1st Tks, on either side of the Tks of each of the 3 cable units, and before final Tks.

Row 73: Bind off in patt (98 sts).

Finishing

Sew all but one panel seam.

Neckband

F Row 1: With smaller hook, pick up 77 loops around neck edge and work 1 R Row.

F Rows 2: Tks across (77 loops).

F Rows 3–5: Tps across (77 loops).

F Row 6: Drop 1st loop from hook, insert hook under selvage stitch of Tks row, 3 rows below, then into dropped loop and pull a loop through all sts. *Insert hook under 1st vertical thread, then, under a corresponding thread in the ridge behind the Tks row, yo and pull a loop through 2 loops; rep from * across row, working the final st under all threads of both selvage sts.

F Rows 7–11: Rep Rows 2–5.

F Row 12: Rep Row 6, binding off by pulling each loop through all loops on hook.

Seam neck band and remaining segment.

Cuffs

Fold poncho in half with neck band seam facing center back.

F Row 1: With RS facing and using a smaller hook pick up 15 loops on each side of the side seam and work 1 R Row (30 loops).

F Row 2: Tks across (30 loops).

F Rows 3–5: Tps across (30 loops).

F Row 6: Drop 1st loop from hook, insert hook under selvage stitch of Tks row 3 rows below then into dropped loop and pull loop through all sts, *insert hook under 1st vertical thread, then, under a corresponding thread in the ridge behind the Tks row, yo and pull a loop through 2 loops; rep from * across row, working the final st under all threads of both selvage sts.

F Rows 7–11: Rep Rows 2–5.

F Row 12: Rep Row 6, binding off by pulling each loop through all lps on hook.

Sew a front to back from base of cuff across next 11 sts on bottom edge. Repeat on opposite side of poncho.

THIS PROJECT WAS CREATED WITH 4 skeins Mountain Colors *Alpaca Blend* in Silverbow, 50% superfine alpaca/50% wool, 7oz/198g = 440yd/402m

Hooks: size 6mm/J–10 standard hook and 6mm/J–10 circular double-ended hook (40"/102cm long) or size needed for gauge*; size 5mm/H–8 hook for trims

8 shank buttons, approx ⅞"/2cm diameter

Approx 3yd/3m leather jewelry cord

Yarn needle

Stitch markers

Shoulder pads (optional)

*You can substitute a 6mm/J–10 Flexi Afghan hook and a 6mm/J–10 standard hook.

STITCHES USED
Chain stitch (ch)

Single crochet (sc)

Extended single crochet (esc)

SPECIAL STITCH TECHNIQUES
Omega Lace crochet is worked in 2 rows

Omega Lace Off row (OLF): Extended sc is the OLF. The OLF row anchors the loops.

To work the OLF row: Ch 1, *insert hook into next st, yo, draw yarn through st (2 loops on hook), yo, draw yarn through 1 loop on hook st (2 loops on hook), yo, draw yarn through 2 loops on hook, remove loop from double-ended hook; rep from * across.

Omega Loop On Row (OLO): This part of the stitch is worked on the flexi double-ended hook. Place a point protector on the end to keep stitches from coming off.

To work the OLO Loop Row: Ch 2, skip 1st esc (Note: loop on the hook counts as the 1st OLO loop), *insert hook in next esc, yo, draw yarn through st and draw up to level of work (approximately 1"/2.5cm); rep from * across row to last st, Insert hook into last st, and draw up a loop to level of work, yo, draw yarn through st, yo, draw through all loops on hook. Ending ch counts as 1 st.

ELEGANT PONCHO • *Designed by Joan A. Davis*

SKILL LEVEL: EXPERIENCED

FINISHED MEASUREMENTS
Women's sizes S (M,L).
Width: 54 (60, 65)"/137 (152, 165)cm from wrist edge to wrist edge.
Length: 38"/97cm from shoulder to bottom edge

YOU WILL NEED
Approx 1278yd/1169m in bulky weight yarn in beige (A)

Approx 568yd/519m bulky weight yarn in burnt orange (B)

Approx 142yd/130m bulky weight yarn in pale orange (C)

The generous shawl collar lifts this poncho into another dimension of elegance.

Pattern

With J-10 hook and A, ch 136 (150, 164).

Row 1 (RS): Working in back bump of ch sts, esc in 2nd ch from hook, esc in each ch across, turn (135 [149, 163] esc).

Left Front

Row 2: Ch 1, esc in each of first 55 (62, 69) esc, turn (55 [62, 69] esc).

Rows 3–4: Ch 1, esc in each esc across, turn (55 [62, 69] esc).

Row 5 (RS) (OLO): With J-10 double-ended hook, ch 2, work OLO in each st across row to last st, in last st, work ending ch, turn (55 [62, 69] loops on hook).

Row 6 (OLF): With opposite end of double-ended hook or J-10 standard hook, insert hook in first loop on double-ended hook, yo, draw yarn through loop, sc in same loop, remove loop from double-ended hook, *esc in next loop on double-ended hook, remove loop from hook; rep from * across to last loop, ending ch in last loop, turn (55 [62, 69] esc).

Rows 7–12: Rep Rows 5-6 (3 times). Complete last st of Row 12 with B. Fasten off A, leaving a 6"/15cm.

Rows 13-16: With B, rep Rows 5-6 (twice). Fasten off B, join C.

Shape Neck

Row 17 (inc row) (OLO): With C, ch 2, 2 OLO in each of next 3 sts, OLO in each esc across to last st, work ending ch in last st, turn (58 [65, 72] loops on hook).

Row 18 (OLF): Rep Row 6 (58 [63, 68] esc). Fasten off C, join B.

Rows 19-22: With B, rep Rows 17-18 (twice) (64 [71, 78] esc at end of Row 22). Fasten off C.

Rows 23-24: With A, rep Rows 17-18 (67 [74, 81] esc at end of Row 24). Fasten off A.

Right Front

Row 2 (OLF): With WS facing, skip next 25 sts to the left of last st made in Row 2 of Left Front, join A in next st, ch 1, esc in each esc across, turn (55 [62, 69] esc).

Rows 3-16: Rep Rows 3-16 of Left Front.

Shape Neck

Row 17 (OLO): Work in OLO pattern across to last 4 sts, 2 OLO in each of next 3 esc, OLO in last esc, turn (58 [65, 72] loops on hook).

Row: 18 (OLF): Rep Row 6 of Left Front (58 [65, 72] esc).

Rows 19-22: With B, rep Rows 17-18 (twice) (64 [71, 78] esc at end of Row 22). Fasten off C.

Rows 23-24: With A, rep Rows 17-18 (67 [74, 81] esc at end of Row 24). Do not fasten off.

Join Fronts

Row 25 (joining row) (OLO): Ch 2, OLO in each esc across to last st on right front, 2 OLO in last esc, working across last row of Left Front, OLO in each esc across to last st, ending ch in last st, turn (135 [149, 163] loops on hook).

Row 26 (OLF): Rep Row 6 of Left Front (135 [149, 163] esc).

Rows 27–36: Rep Rows 5-6 of Left Front (5 times). Fasten off.

Center Front

Row 37 (OLO): With RS facing, skip first 35 sts, join A in next st, ch 2, OLO in each of next 63 (77, 91 esc), ending ch in next esc, turn leaving rem sts unworked (65 [79, 93] loops on hook).

Row 38 (OLF): Rep Row 6 of Left Front (65 [79, 93] esc).

Rows 39-60: Rep Rows 5-6 of Left Front (11 times) (65 [79, 93] esc). Fasten off A.

Back

Row 2 (OLF): With WS of Poncho facing, working across opposite side of foundation ch, join A in first ch, ch 1, esc in each ch across to last ch, turn (135 [149, 163] esc).

Rows 3-4: Ch 1, esc in each esc across, turn (135 [149, 163] esc).

Rows 5-12: Rep Rows 5-6 of Left Front (4 times) (135 [149, 163] esc). Fasten off A, join B.

Rows 13–36: Rep Rows 5-6 in the following color sequence: 4 rows B, 2 rows C, 4 rows B, 14 rows A (135 [149, 163] esc). Fasten off A.

Center Back

Rep Rows 37–60 of center front. Fasten off A.

Neck Edging

Rnd 1: With RS facing, using J-10 standard hook, join A in center st on Back neck edge, ch 1, esc in each of next 12 sts across Back neck edge, working in row-end sts across Left Front neck edge, (sc2tog in next 2 sts) twice, work 14 esc evenly spaced across A section to next B stripe, complete last st with B, drop A to WS to be picked up later, working over A strand, *with B, work 6 esc across B stripe, drop B to be picked up later, join C, working over A and B strands, with C, work 3 esc across C stripe, fasten off C, pick up B, with B, work 6 esc across B stripe, fasten off B, pick up A*, with A, sc2tog (twice) worked across next 2 rows to center front point of neck opening, with A, sc2tog (twice) worked across next 2 rows on Right Front neck edge, drop A, join a separate strand of B, rep from * to * once, with A, work 14 esc across to last 2 rows before Back neck edge, sc2tog (twice)

worked across next 2 rows, working across Back neck edge, esc in each of next 12 sts, sl st in first esc to join (90 sts).

Rnd 2: With H-8 hook, ch 1, esc evenly around, working in matching colors, and working 2 decs at each inside corner, sl st in first esc to join (84 esc). Fasten off A.

Work now progresses in rows.

Shawl Collar

Row 3: With H-8 hook and A, loosely ch 17, with RS facing, esc in first st to the left of center front V, esc in each st around, ending at last st before V at center front V, ch 18, turn (84 esc; ch-17 length on one side; ch-18 length on other side).

Row 4: Esc in 2nd ch from hook, esc in each of next 16 ch, esc in each esc across Collar, esc in each of next 17 ch, turn (118 esc).

Rows 5–6: Ch 1, esc in each esc across, turn (118 esc).

Row 7: Ch 1, esc in first 3 esc, 2 esc in next esc, esc in each of next 23 esc, 2 esc in next esc, esc in next 19 esc, 2 esc in next esc, *esc in next 11 esc, 2 esc in next esc; rep from * once, esc in next 19 esc. 2 esc in next esc, esc in next 23 esc, 2 esc in next esc, esc in last 3 esc, turn (125 esc).

Row 8: Ch 1, esc in each esc across, turn (125 esc).

Row 9 (OLO): With J-10 double-ended hook, ch 2, OLO in each esc across to last st, ending ch in last st, turn (125 loops on hook).

Row 10 (OLF): With J-10 standard hook, work in OLF pattern across (rep Row 6 of left front) (125 esc). Fasten off A, leaving a long sewing length, join B.

Row 11–16: Rep Rows 9-10 (3 times) working in the following color sequence, leaving a sewing length when fastening off each color: 2 rows B; 2 rows C; 2 rows B. Do not fasten off.

Collar Finishing

Row 1: Fold Collar in half, with RS facing, matching sts across row-end sts of Rows 4–16, working through double thickness and using J-10 standard hook and matching color yarn, ch 1, *2 sc in row-end esc, ch 2, skip next OLO row-end st; rep from * twice, sc in each of next 7 row-end sts, turn.

Row 2: Ch 1, sc in evenly across, matching colors. Fasten off all colors.

Finishing

Rnd 1: With J-10 standard hook, attach yarn at Back Left underarm, ch 1, ** *work 2 sc in next row-end esc, ch 2, skip next OLO row-end st*, rep from * to * along side edge to bottom corner, (2 sc, ch 1, 2 sc) in corner st, sc in each st across bottom edge, (2 sc, ch 1, 2 sc) in corner st, rep from * to * across side edge to next inside corner, sc in each st across bottom edge of sleeve to next corner, (2 sc, ch 1, 2 sc) in corner st, working across side edge, matching colors, rep from * to * across to Row 4, sc in each row end st across shoulder seam to Row 4 of Front, rep from * to * across to bottom corner, matching colors, (2 sc, ch 1, 2 sc) in corner st, sc in each st across bottom edge of sleeve to next corner; rep from ** around, sl st in first sc to join. Fasten off all colors.

Left Side Buttonhole Edging

With RS facing, using J-10 standard hook, join A in bottom right-hand corner of Center Front, ch 1, sc in first sc, *2 sc in next ch-2 sp, sc in next sc*; rep from * to * 5 times, (sc, ch 6, sc) in next ch-2 sp (buttonhole made), sc in next sc, rep from * to * 3 times, (sc, ch 6, sc) in next ch-2 sp (buttonhole made), sc in next sc, 2 sc in next ch-2 space, working across bottom edge of sleeve, sc in each st across to next corner. Fasten off.

Right Side Buttonhole Edging

With RS facing, using J-10 standard hook, join A in corner on bottom edge of right sleeve underarm edge, ch 1, sc in each st across to next corner, working down left side edge of center front, 2 sc in next ch-2 sp, sc in next sc, (sc, ch 6, sc) in next ch-2 sp (buttonhole made), sc in next sc, *2 sc in next ch-2 sp, sc in next sc*; rep from * to * 3 times, (sc, ch 6, sc) in next ch-2 sp (buttonhole made), sc in next sc, rep from * to * 6 times. Fasten off.

Repeat left and right side buttonhole edgings on back.

Button Sets (make 4)

Attach leather cord to button with a knot. Run cord through second button about 2"/5cm below 1st button. Knot and cut off cord. Attach one button set in matching buttonholes on front and back sides.

Weave in ends and remove all stitch markers.

THIS PROJECT WAS CREATED WITH

A: 9 skeins of Patons *Divine* in Soft Earth (#06011), 79.5% acrylic/18% mohair/2.5% polyester, 3½oz/100g = 142yd/129m

B: 4 skeins of Patons *Divine* in Floral Fantasy (#06740), 79.5% acrylic/18% mohair/2.5% polyester, 3½oz/100g = 142yd/129m

C: 1 skein of Patons *Divine* in Orangina (#06605), 79.5% acrylic/18% mohair/2.5% polyester, 3½oz/100g = 142yd/129m

Large lacy square motifs come together to create this distinctive poncho. The bold, rich color palette is a contemporary choice for this stylish flashback.

MARRAKECH EXPRESS PONCHO • *Designed by Katherine Lee*

First Square

Ch 5, and close into a ring with 1 sl st in first ch.

Rnd 1: Ch 9 (counts as tr, ch 5), (tr, ch 5) 7 times in ring. Sl st in 4th ch of beg ch 9 (8 ch-5 loops)

Rnd 2: Sl st in 1st ch-5 sp, ch 1, (3 sc, ch 3, 3 sc) in each ch-5 loop around. Sl st in first sc to join (8 ch-3 sps).

Rnd 3: Sl st to 1st ch-3 sp, ch 6 (counts as dc, ch 3), dc in same ch-3 sp, *ch 3, (3 dc, ch 3, 3 dc) in next ch-3 sp, ch 3, (dc, ch 3, dc) in next ch-3 sp; rep from * twice, ch 3, (3 dc, ch 3, 3 dc) in next ch-3 sp, ch 3. Sl st in 3rd ch of turning ch to join (12 ch-3 sps)

Rnd 4: Sl st in 1st ch-3 sp, ch 4 (counts as tr), (2 tr, ch 5, 3 tr) in same ch-3 sp, *ch 7, skip next ch-3 sp, sc in next ch-3 sp, ch 7, skip next ch-3 sp, (3 tr, ch 5, 3 tr) in next ch-3 sp; rep from * twice, ch 7, skip next ch-3 sp, sc in next ch-3 sp, ch 7. Sl st in 3rd ch of turning ch to join (4 ch-5 corner loops).

Rnd 5: Ch 1, sc in same ch as joining sl st, sc in each of next 2 tr, *(3 sc, ch 3, 3 sc) in next ch-5 loop, sc in each of next 3 tr, 7 sc in next ch-7 loop, ch 1, 7 sc in next ch-7 loop, sc in each of next 3 tr; rep from * twice, (3 sc, ch 3, 3 sc) in next ch-5 loop, sc in each of

SKILL LEVEL: ADVANCED

FINISHED MEASUREMENTS
One size fits most
Neck edge: 21"/53cm circumference
Length: 29"/74cm from neck edge to center front point (excluding fringe)

YOU WILL NEED
Approx 882yd/807m of worsted weight yarn
Hook: size 5.5mm/I–9 or size needed to obtain gauge

STITCHES USED
Chain stitch (ch)
Double crochet (dc)
Single crochet (sc)
Slip stitch (sl st)
Treble crochet (tr)

SPECIAL STITCH TECHNIQUE
Treble crochet decrease (tr2tog): Yo twice, insert hook in next st, yo, draw yarn through 2 loops on hook (twice)

GAUGE
Take time to check your gauge.
Rnds 1–4 of square = 4"/10cm in diameter
Each square = 10¼"/26cm square

next 3 tr, 7 sc in next ch-7 loop, ch 1, 7 sc in next ch-7 loop. Sl st in 3rd ch of turning ch to join (4 ch-3 corner sps).

Rnd 6: Ch 1, sc in 1st sc, ch 5, * (dc, ch 5, dc, ch 7, dc, ch 5, dc) in next ch-3 sp, ch 5, skip next 5 sc, sc in next sc, ch 5, skip next 3 sc, sc in next sc, ch 5, sc in next ch-1 sp, ch 5, skip next 3 sc, sc in next sc**, ch 5, skip next 3 sc, sc in next sc, ch 5; rep from * twice, rep from * to ** once, ch 2, dc to 1st sc instead of last loop of ch-5 (4 ch-7 corner loops).

Rnd 7: Ch 1, sc in 1st loop, * ch 3, skip next ch-5 loop, (3 tr, ch 5, 3 tr) in 3rd ch of next ch-5 loop, (3 tr, ch 9, 3 tr) in 4th ch of next ch-7 loop, (3 tr, ch 5, 3 tr) in 3rd ch of next ch-5 loop, ch 3, skip next ch-5 loop, sc in next ch-5 loop, ch 3, 3 tr in 3rd ch of next ch-5 loop, ch 5, work tr2tog, working first tr in same ch as last tr made and 2nd tr in 3rd ch of next ch-5 loop, yo and draw through all 3 loops on hook, ch 5, 3 tr in same ch as last tr, ch 3**, sc in next ch-5 loop; rep from * twice, rep from * to ** once. Sl st in 1st sc to join (4 ch-9 corner loops).

Second and Successive Squares

Make 11 more squares same as first square, joining each to previous square(s) with 1 sl st in each ch-9 corner loop and each ch-5 side loop while completing last rnd.

Replace each ch-9 corner loop to be joined with ch 4, sl st in corresponding ch-9 corner loop of previous square, ch 4; replace each ch-5 loop on side to be joined with ch 2, sl st in corresponding ch-5 loop on previous Square, ch 2.

Neck Edging

Rnd 1: With RS facing, join yarn to top back neck edge at junction of 3 Squares, ch 1, sc in junction, *4 sc in next ch-4 sp, sc in each of next 6 tr, 5 sc in ch-5 loop, sc in each of next 3 tr, 3 sc in each of next 2 ch-3 sps, sc in each of next 3 tr, 5 sc in in each of next 2 ch-5 sps, sc in each of next 3 tr, 3 sc in each of next 2 ch-3 sps, sc in each of next 3 tr, 5 sc in ch-5 loop, sc in each of next 6 tr, 4 sc in next ch-4 sp*, sc in next junction of 3 Squares; rep from * to * once. Sl st in 1st sc to join. Fasten off.

Fringe

Cut 15"/38cm lengths of yarn for fringe. Using 3 strands for each fringe, attach 1 fringe to each ch-3, ch-4, and ch-5 loop around bottom edge.

Fold strands in half. Insert hook in loop, put folded strands over hook pulling through slightly. With folded strand remaining on hook, yarn over and pull yarn ends through fold.

Drawstring Tie
Ch 2.

Row 1: Sc in 2nd ch from hook, turn (1 sc).

Row 2: Ch 1, sc in sc, turn (1 sc).

Rep row 2 until tie measures 52"/132cm from beg. Fasten off.

Starting and ending at center front, weave drawstring tie through spaces along top edge.

Attach fringe to each end of drawstring tie.

THIS PROJECT WAS CREATED WITH 9 balls of *Karabella* Yarns *Aurora 8* in Pumpkin (#704), 100% Merino Wool, 1¾oz/50g = 98yd/90m

The Hook

In the directions for each poncho in this book and for any other crochet pattern you might work on, you'll be instructed to use a specific hook size. Whether you use an aluminum, plastic, or wooden hook is a matter of personal preference. What matters is the size of the hook—it determines the stitch size and, to some extent, the gauge (number of stitches per inch) that the pattern is based on.

In addition to regular crochet hooks, you may be instructed to use a Tunisian or Afghan hook (for Tunisian crochet) or a circular crochet hook (for the Omega Lace technique). These hooks are longer than regular crochet hooks for a reason: Stitches are left on the hook as you work across a row.

Tools and Materials

Aside from some luscious yarn, you simply need a hook to create a poncho. That's it! Of course, there are always a few tools that are handy and helpful to have, but they aren't essential. You may have some of them stashed away among your sewing or crafting tools.

You will encounter three different systems of hook sizes when you start to purchase hooks. The Continental (European) system uses millimeters, the U.S. (American) system uses a combination letter/number system, and the United Kingdom uses a numeric system. The hook sizes listed in the projects are of the Continental and U.S. systems (see page 126).

Additional Tools

Scissors, especially small ones with sharp points, are indispensable tools. Breaking yarn is not an efficient way to cut yarn. Always use scissors.

Stitch markers are handy when you need to mark the end of a row in your work or a specific stitch within a row. If you don't wish to purchase stitch markers, use a safety pin or a short length of contrasting yarn to mark your spot.

Rulers and cloth tape measures with both standard and metric measurements are useful tools that you probably already have. You will use these tools to measure your work as you progress, to check your gauge (see page 121), and to measure finished pieces as you finish and block them.

Rust-proof pins of all types—straight pins, T-pins, and safety pins—all have their uses. Make absolutely sure that any type of pin you choose to use is rust-proof. T-pins are useful for blocking (see page 123) and safety pins can be used as stitch markers. Straight pins are great for securing crocheted pieces together as you stitch them and later, as you block them.

Yarn needles with large eyes and blunt points are necessary for finishing a crochet project. Using a plastic or metal needle is a matter of preference. Use them to weave loose yarn ends back into your stitches, or to sew together the seams of a garment.

Bags make it easy for you to take your crochet anywhere and everywhere you go. You may choose to tuck your current project, yarn, and a few tools in a plastic grocery bag or invest in a stylish, multipurpose needlework tote. Just be sure your bag doesn't have any tiny holes your hooks or pins might slip through.

Yarn

Variety, luxury, and novelty are some of the buzzwords you encounter when reading about yarn today. The range of different types of yarn is, simply put, mind-boggling. If you've never shopped for yarn, you may easily be overwhelmed as you look for material for a specific project (pleasantly so, I might add). Give in to the addictive pleasure of acquisition; don't resist it! After all, you can always find a way to use the yarn sooner or later.

Each project in this book lists a generic yarn type to use. In addition, each project lists the manufacturer, style, and color of the specific yarn used to create the project. Pay attention to the type of yarn specified for each project and, if you wish to use a yarn other than the one the designer used (see Substituting Yarn on page 122), look for that type of yarn.

For the purpose of this book, yarn or thread are catchall terms for any fiberlike material used for crochet, even when you're crocheting with ribbon, cloth, or other materials.

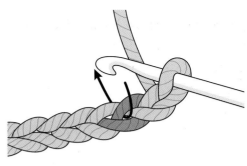

figure 1

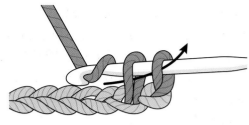

figure 3

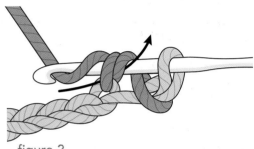

figure 2

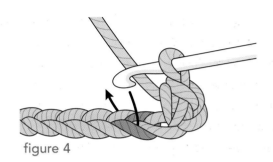

figure 4

Basic Crochet Stitches

If you're wondering how many yo's to make for a triple treble crochet, you're in the right place. Here you'll find step-by-step, illustrated explanations for all of the stitches used to create the ponchos in this book. You'll also find step-by-step explanations for out-of-the-ordinary stitches and techniques you may need, such as Tunisian crochet, front and back post crochet, and the Omega Lace technique.

Single Crochet

Single crochet (sc) is a short, basic stitch. Work this stitch into a foundation chain of any number of stitches.

1. Find the second chain stitch from the crochet hook. Insert the point of the hook under the two top loops of the chain stitch (figure 1).

2. Bring the yarn over the crochet hook, catch the yarn and pull it through the loop on the hook (figure 2). You will now have two loops on your hook.

3. Bring the yarn over the hook again, grab the yarn with the hook, and pull the yarn through both loops (figure 3). You've completed your first single crochet stitch.

4. Insert your hook in the next chain stitch and repeat the steps to create another single crochet (figure 4).

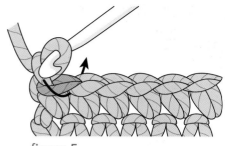

figure 5

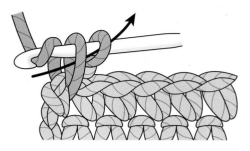

figure 7

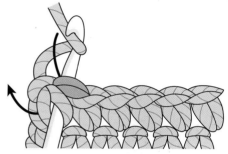

figure 6

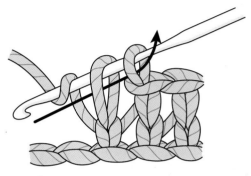

figure 8

Reverse Single Crochet

Just as the name implies, you work this stitch just as you do a regular single crochet—except in reverse, from left to right. This stitch is used most frequently for creating a finished edge on completed work.

1. Work this stitch with the right side of your work facing you. Insert the hook from front to back in the stitch to the right of your hook (figure 5).

2. Bring the yarn over the hook and pull the yarn through the stitch (figure 6).

3. Yarn over and bring the yarn through both loops. You've completed one reverse single crochet (figure 7). Continue to work back across the row and fasten off the yarn at the end of the row.

Extended Single Crochet

Extended single crochet (esc) is also referred to as locked single crochet or knotted single crochet. It's used as a basis for the Omega Lace technique (see page 93).

1. Insert hook into the bump side of the foundation chain. Yarn over and pull the loop through. You'll have two loops on your hook.

2. Yarn over, pull through 1 loop on the hook; yo, pull through 2 loops on the hook to the desired height (figure 8).

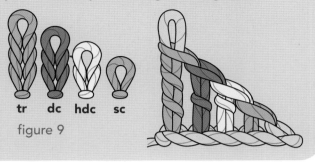

figure 11

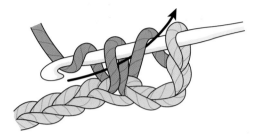

figure 12

figure 13

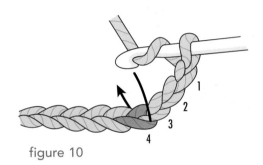

figure 10

Double Crochet

Double crochet (dc) is the workhorse stitch of many crochet patterns. It's about twice as tall as the single crochet stitch. Combining the double crochet stitch with other stitches produces different patterns and textures.

1. Make a foundation chain of any number of stitches. Bring the yarn over the hook and insert the hook into the fourth chain from the hook (figure 10).

2. Bring the yarn over the hook and pull the yarn through the chain stitch. You'll have three loops on your hook (figure 11).

3. Bring the yarn over the hook and draw the yarn through the first two loops on the hook (figure 12). You'll have two loops on your hook.

4. Bring the yarn over the hook once more, then pull the yarn through the last two loops on your hook

figure 14

(figure 13). You've completed one double crochet stitch. You'll have one loop left on your hook to start your next double crochet.

5. Bring the yarn over your hook, insert your hook in the next stitch (figure 14), and continue across the row. At the end of the row, turn your work and chain three to make your turning chain.

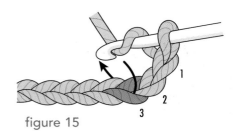

figure 15

figure 17

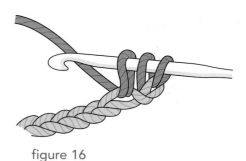

figure 16

figure 18

Half Double Crochet

The half double crochet (hdc) is slightly shorter than a double crochet and taller than a single crochet. To start, make a foundation chain of any number of stitches.

1. Bring the yarn over the hook, locate the third chain stitch from the hook (figure 15), and insert the hook in the chain.

2. Bring the yarn over the hook and catch it with the hook. Pull the hook through the chain. You should have three loops on the hook (figure 16).

3. Bring the yarn over the hook, catch the yarn with the hook, and pull it through the three loops on the hook (figure 17).

4. You will have one loop left on the hook. You've created one half double crochet stitch (figure 18). Yarn over and insert the hook in the next chain and repeat the sequence across the row.

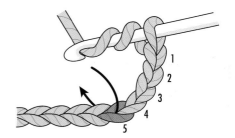

figure 19

figure 20

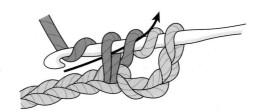

figure 21

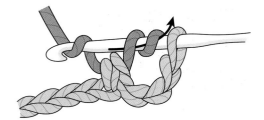

figure 22

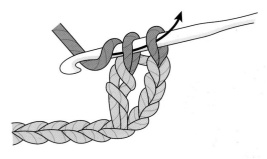

figure 23

figure 24

Treble Crochet

Treble crochet (tr) is taller than double crochet. It's often used to create an open, lacey fabric.

Start with a foundation chain of any number of stitches.

1. Identify the fifth chain stitch from the hook. Bring the yarn over the hook twice (figure 19).

2. Insert the hook into the fifth chain. Bring the yarn over the hook, catch the yarn, and pull the hook through the chain. You'll have four loops on the hook (figure 20).

3. Bring the yarn over the hook, catch the yarn, and slide the hook through the first two loops (figure 21).

4. Yarn over the hook and draw your yarn through the next two loops on the hook (figure 22).

5. Yarn over the hook and draw the yarn through the last two loops on your hook (figure 23).

6. You will end up with only one loop on your hook. You've completed one treble crochet stitch (figure 24). Yarn over twice and repeat the steps in the next chain stitch.

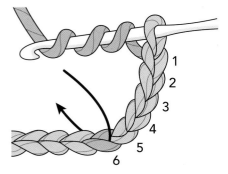

figure 25

figure 26

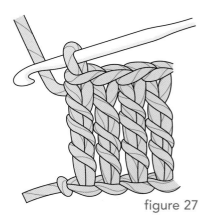

figure 27

Double Treble

The double treble crochet (dtr) is even taller than a treble crochet. This stitch is best used to create a very loose, openwork fabric.

Make a foundation chain of any number of stitches, then chain five additional stitches for a turning chain.

1. Yarn over the hook three times. Insert the hook in the sixth chain from the hook (figure 25). Yarn over the hook.

2. Gently pull the wrapped hook through the center of the stitch carrying the wrapped yarn through the stitch. You will have five loops on your hook.

3. Yarn over the hook. Draw the yarn through the first two loops on your hook. Repeat this step three more times until you have only one loop on the hook. Start your next dtr by bringing the yarn over three times and inserting the hook in the next chain of the foundation row (figure 26).

4. At the end of the row (figure 27), make five chains to start another row of dtr.

Triple Treble

The triple treble stitch (trtr) is worked just as you work any other triple stitch. And yes, there are even double triple trebles and quadruple triple trebles—you simply increase the number of times you yarn over to make these really tall stitches.

1. Yarn over the hook four times. Insert the hook in the seventh chain from the hook (figure 28). Yarn over the hook.

2. Gently pull the wrapped hook through the center of the stitch carrying the wrapped yarn through the stitch. You will have six loops on your hook.

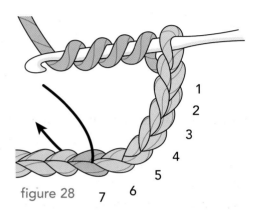

figure 28   1 2 3 4 5 6 7

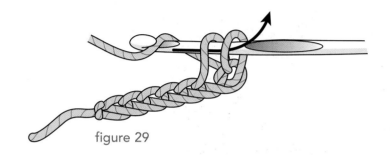

figure 29

3. Yarn over the hook. Draw the yarn through the first two loops on your hook. Repeat this step four more times until you have only one loop on the hook. Start your next trtr by bringing the yarn over four times and inserting the hook in the next chain of the foundation row.

4. At the end of the row, make six chains to start another row of trtr.

Slip Stitch

The slip stitch (sl st) is a versatile and functional stitch. Use this stitch to create a firm finished edge or to join two finished crocheted pieces. Use a slip stitch to join a new skein of yarn to your crochet project or when you change yarn color. Combine the slip stitch with other stitches to form fancy stitches that look complicated.

As versatile as it is, the slip stitch is most commonly used to join one end of a foundation chain to the opposite end, forming a ring. The ring then forms the foundation for working pieces in the round.

To make a slip stitch, insert your hook into a stitch. Yarn over the hook and draw the yarn through the stitch and the loop on your hook. You'll have one loop left on your hook (figure 29).

Special Techniques & Stitches

The following stitches are not used in every project but are useful stitches to know and fun to experiment with. Refer to this section if the pattern you're working calls for any of these special stitches.

Tunisian Crochet

Tunisian crochet—also called tricot crochet, railroad knitting, or Afghan stitch—is a variation of standard crochet with two primary differences.

One difference between standard crochet and Tunisian crochet is the size of the hook used: A much longer hook is used to create the work (see photo) because in Tunisian crochet, you work a single row in two parts. As you work the first part of each row, the loops you make are kept on the hook (that's why you use a longer hook). Working the second part of the row takes the loops off your hook. The fabric created with Tunisian crochet has a distinctive look that differs from standard crochet.

Tunisian Simple Stitch

Tunisian simple stitch (Tss) is begun with a foundation chain of ordinary chain stitches.

1. Insert your hook into the second chain from the hook (figure 30). Bring the yarn over the hook and draw the yarn through. You will have two loops on your hook.

2. Insert your hook into the next chain, bring the yarn over, and draw the yarn through. You've added another loop to your hook. As you work, you'll have one loop on your hook for each chain stitch in your foundation chain (figure 31).

3. To work the second half of the row, bring the yarn over the hook and draw it through one loop on the hook (figure 32).

4. Bring the yarn over the hook; draw it through the next two loops on the hook. Bring the yarn over again, draw it through two loops. Continue across the row until only one loop remains on the hook (figure 33).

figure 30

figure 31

5. To start your next row, insert your hook behind the next vertical bar in the row below (figure 34). Bring the yarn over the hook and draw the yarn through the stitch. Continue across the row, keeping all the loops on your hook (figure 35).

6. Work the return row as you did in steps 3 and 4: Bringing the yarn first through one loop, then completing the row by bringing the yarn through two loops at a time across the row.

Tunisian Slip Stitch

Tunisian slip stitch (Tsl) is worked in the following manner.

1. Insert the hook into a stitch as you would when you work Tunisian simple stitch, but do not yarn over or pull the yarn through the stitch (figure 36).

figure 32

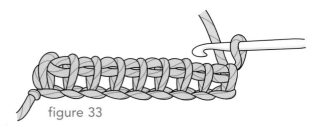

figure 33

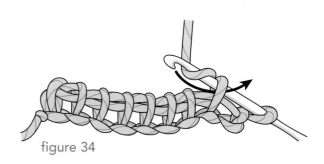

figure 34

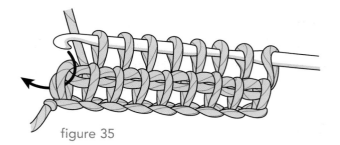

figure 35

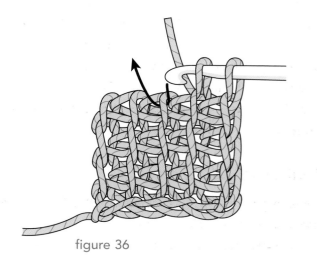

figure 36

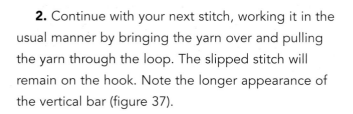

figure 37

2. Continue with your next stitch, working it in the usual manner by bringing the yarn over and pulling the yarn through the loop. The slipped stitch will remain on the hook. Note the longer appearance of the vertical bar (figure 37).

Tunisian Knit Stitch

Tunisian knit stitch (Tks) is a nice variation for Tunisian crochet. This stitch creates a fabric that looks very much like knitted fabric with rows of little V-shaped stitches. You begin this stitch with a completed foundation row of Tunisian stitch (Tss).

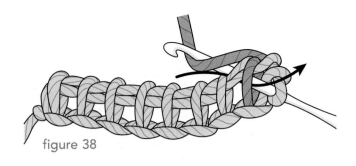

figure 38

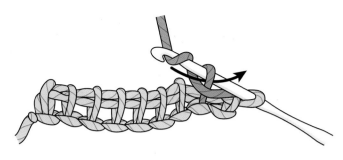

figure 41

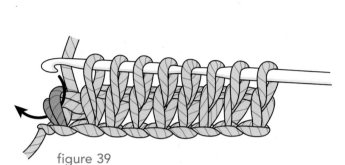

figure 39

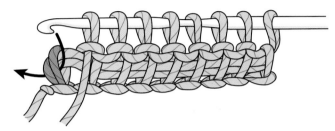

figure 42

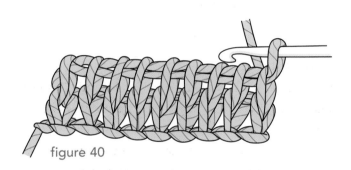

figure 40

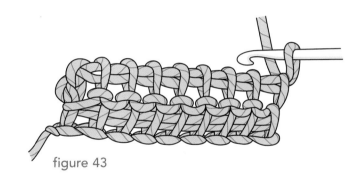

figure 43

1. Insert the hook from front to back, between the front and back strands of the next vertical stitch. Yarn over. Draw the yarn through the stitch. Work across the row to the next-to-last-stitch (figure 38).

2. Insert the hook under the last 2 vertical bars at the end of the row. Yarn over and draw the yarn through the stitch (figure 39).

3. Work the return row as you would a regular return row (see page 114). The completed first row of Tks is shown in figure 40.

Tunisian Purl Stitch

The Tunisian purl stitch (Tps) is often used with other Tunisian stitches to produce textured patterns. Like Tunisian knit stitch, you begin with a completed foundation row.

1. Bring the working yarn to the front of your work. Insert the hook under the next vertical stitch, but behind the strand of yarn you are working with.

2. Yarn over, bring the yarn through the stitch (figure 41).

3. At the end of the row, yarn over and bring the yarn through the stitch (figure 42). Work the second half of the row just as you would Tss (see page 114). Figure 43 shows a completed row of Tsp.

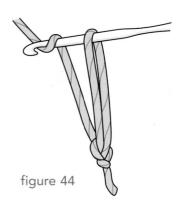

figure 44

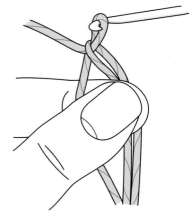

figure 45

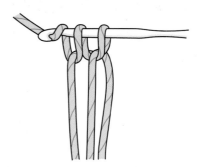

figure 46

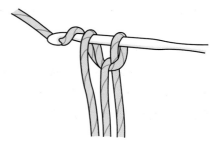

figure 47

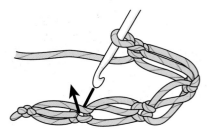

figure 48

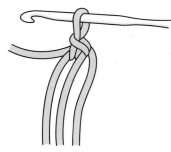

figure 49

Solomon's Knot

This special stitch is simply a lengthened chain stitch locked in place with a single crochet stitch worked into the back loop.

1. Make one chain and lengthen the loop as directed in your pattern. Wrap the yarn over your hook (figure 44).

2. Pull the yarn through the hook. Grasp the two front threads of your chain with your fingers, separating them from the back thread (figure 45).

3. Position the hook under the single thread and bring the thread over the hook (figure 46).

4. Draw the yarn through and bring the thread over once more (figure 47).

5. Draw both loops on the hook to complete the stitch (figure 48).

6. To create a fabric composed of Solomon's knots, you will need to work back into the knots in the lengthened chains (figure 49).

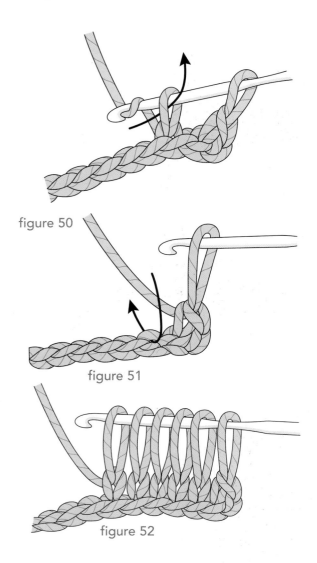

figure 50

figure 51

figure 52

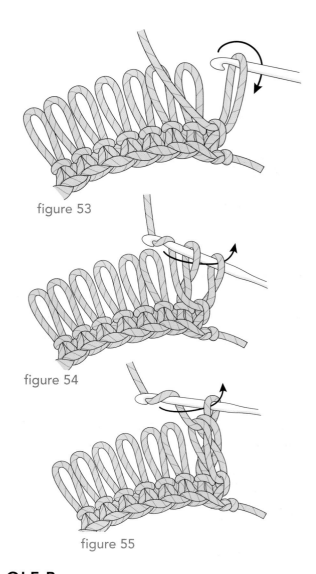

figure 53

figure 54

figure 55

Omega Lace

Omega lace is based on loop stitch (lp st) and extended single crochet (ex sc). It is worked in two distinct rows: Omega loops on row (OLO) and an Omega lace off row (OLF).

OLO Row

1. Insert hook into the bump side of the foundation chain. Yarn over and pull the loop through. You'll have two loops on your hook (figure 50).

2. Yarn over, pull through 1 loop on the hook (figure 51); yo, pull through 2 loops on the hook to the desired height. Continue across the row holding the loops on your hook (figure 52).

OLF Row

1. Slide a long loop onto the hook. Chain one and slip hook back into the loop. Yarn over, pull through the loop; there are two loops on the hook. Yarn over, pull through one loop, then yarn over and pull through booth loops in one motion (figure 53).

2. Insert hook into next loop; yarn over and pull through one loop (figure 54).

3. Yarn over, pull through both loops in one motion (figure 55).

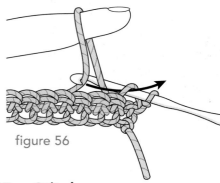

figure 56

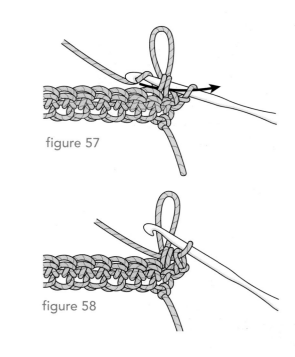

figure 57

figure 58

Loop/Fur Stitch

This stitch is simply another variation of single crochet. It is usually worked on wrong side rows because the loops form at the back of the crocheted fabric. The long loops that are created make an interesting looped fabric. If desired, you can cut the loops to subtly change the texture of the fabric.

1. Use the left-hand finger to control the size of the loop. Insert the hook, pick up both threads of the loop, and draw them through (figure 56).

2. Wrap the yarn over the hook (figure 57) and draw through all of the loops on the hook to complete the stitch (figure 58).

Back and Front Post Double Crochet

You can create raised patterns that resemble ribbing or even intricate cables using post stitches. The way you insert your hook around a post—back post (BP) or front post (FP)—determines the look of the stitch. You'll be given specific instructions in your pattern if you need to use this technique to create a stitch (figures 59 and 60).

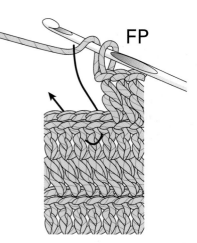

FP

figure 59

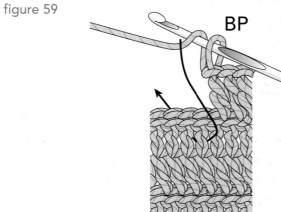

BP

figure 60

Basic Shaping Techniques

Working only a rectangle or circle of crochet could be mind numbing and not very useful. There are only so many things you can do with either of those shapes. Simply by adding or subtracting the number of stitches in a row, you can shape the fabric you're creating.

It's very important to count stitches as you increase or decrease according to your pattern. Take time to count your stitches, and then count them again!

Increasing

Increasing stitches are simply added stitches worked into a row. Your pattern will tell you when and where to increase (inc). It may be at the beginning, end, or even the middle of the row you're working on. No matter where the increase appears, simply working a given number of stitches into a single stitch makes an increase.

Working an increase at the beginning or end of a row is the most common method to add stitches: It gives your fabric a smooth edge. In the example shown, a double crochet increase is worked into the first stitch (figure 61). (Remember: Your turning chain counts as the first stitch!) Figure 62 illustrates a double crochet increase in the middle of a row.

Decreasing

Decreasing is simply a way to subtract stitches in a row. A decrease (dec) can be worked at the beginning, end, or middle of a row. Your pattern will tell you precisely where and how to make a decrease. In short, to decrease you combine two separate stitches into one stitch.

Read your pattern directions carefully so you understand how to work decreases successfully.

For a decrease in double crochet, work a double crochet until you have two loops on your hook. Yarn over your hook and insert it in the next stitch. Yarn over, draw the yarn through the stitch, yarn over, and draw the yarn through the first two loops on your

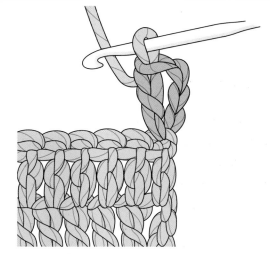

figure 61

figure 62

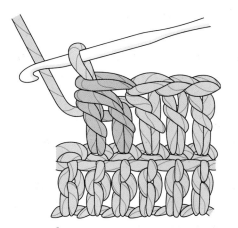

figure 63

hook. Yarn over and draw the yarn through all three loops on your hook.

In the example shown (figure 63), a decrease has been worked in double crochet. If you look at the tops of the stitches, you will see only one stitch crossing the top of two stitch posts.

Reading a Pattern

Have you found a half dozen ponchos in this book (or more) that you want to make for yourself or for gifts? All you need to do is gather the materials and follow the pattern instructions.

Written patterns provide a lot of important information before you actually pick up your hook and yarn. Reading a pattern from beginning to end before you crochet isn't an optional step, it's required—and it simply makes sense.

Here's the information you'll find in crochet patterns for this book and other books or magazines.

Experience Level

A pattern will tell you which level of experience it's designed for: beginner, easy, intermediate, or experienced. Pay attention to the level of experience needed to create a project, and then read through the pattern just to be sure it's right for you.

Beginners will use basic stitches in a straightforward manner. There will be minimal shaping of the project.

Easy patterns use basic stitches, simple repetitive stitch patterns, simple color changes, and easy-to-master shaping and finishing techniques.

Intermediate patterns use a variety of stitches and more complex stitch patterns. Lace patterns and complex color changes may also be used.

Experienced level patterns use intricate stitch patterns, work from charted stitches, use finer threads, smaller hooks, and detailed shaping and finishing.

Size or Dimensions

A pattern will give you the sizes the garment is designed for or the finished dimensions of a project or project component.

Materials and Tools

Every pattern will list the materials, the specific hook size, and other tools you'll need. The pattern will tell you exactly which type of yarn is used and approximately how much you'll need to create the project. In most cases, the pattern will tell you the specific brand of yarn used to crochet the project.

Stitch List

The stitches used in the pattern will be listed with their abbreviations (see page 126). If advanced or specialty stitches are used, you'll be given directions for the stitches. If special changes in standard stitch construction or unique working methods are used, those changes will be noted and brought to your attention before you start.

Gauge

A gauge will be specified for the design. Pay attention to the gauge. If you want your project to be the size you intend it to be, make a gauge sample before you start on the project.

Gauge is measured by stitches or rows of stitches per inch. If your project is made solely with single crochet, you'll use single crochet stitches to make the sample. If the project has a set of several different stitches that repeat across the row, you'll need to create a sample for that set of stitches.

Create a gauge sample that measures 4 x 4 inches (10 x 10 cm) or larger. It's imperative that you create your sample with the same yarn and hook you plan to use to crochet the project.

If your sample doesn't result in the specified gauge, rework another sample with a larger (or smaller) hook size or adjust your stitch tension as you crochet until your sample matches the required gauge. It's as simple as that.

Instructions, Pattern Notes, and Graphs

Every pattern will be written with step-by-step instructions beginning with the number of chain stitches you need for your foundation row. Then it will continue with row-by-row descriptions of the stitches or pattern stitches that you'll work to complete the poncho. If the project is made with more than one piece, each piece will be given separate step-by-step directions.

If there are special stitch variations or unusual working methods for the pattern, these will be noted in a separate section of pattern notes or working notes.

If there are specific color changes that make up a pattern for checks or stripes, these changes may be shown graphically with an illustration or a charted graph. Each square on a charted graph will be equal to a given number of stitches.

Finishing and Assembly

If your poncho needs to be blocked (shaped) or assembled, the instructions will tell you what to do and, in some cases, how to do it.

In addition, if a poncho needs button loops, fringe, pom-poms, or other embellishments you'll be given instructions on how to create each one as needed.

Substituting Yarn

Does the color orange make your skin look pallid? Are you allergic to mohair? Don't feel constrained by a designer's choice of color or yarn. Substitute your own choice of color or material for the same type of yarn called for in the pattern. If you've never done this before, here are four easy steps to help you make your poncho truly your own.

1. Identify the yarn type that the pattern calls for. Yarn companies classify each of their yarns by weight or size (yarn thickness). There's some crossover between types, but in general they're separated into six distinct groups: superfine yarns, fine yarns, light yarns, medium weight yarns, bulky, and super bulky yarns.

Once you know the type of yarn you need, you'll look for a similar type of yarn that suits your needs and desires. Most—if not all—yarns have the yarn type printed on the label. But don't go shopping yet.

2. Determine the total amount of yarn necessary to create the project. Jot down the total length of each ball of the original yarn in the pattern. Multiply the number of balls called for by yards/meters per ball. This will tell you how much yarn you need. Write down the total amount of each yarn type you will need for the project.

3. Here's the fun part—go to your local yarn shop, craft store, or visit the myriad of yarn suppliers online. When you find the yarn you want to use, divide the total yardage you need by the yards/meters per ball of the new yarn you have chosen. Round up to the next whole number (you don't want to run short of yarn!). This will give you the number of skeins of the substitute yarn that you need..

4. Finally, crochet a gauge sample with the recommended hook and the yarn you've purchased. Don't skip this step! If the gauge is accurate, crochet away.

Those Finishing Touches

You've made the very last stitch in your poncho, but you're not finished yet! Here are some techniques you'll need to finish off your project.

Fastening Off

When you've come to the end of your pattern and made your very last stitch, you'll need to cut your skein of yarn from the crocheted fabric. If you don't fasten the yarn properly, the sight of an unraveling poncho will cause you to cry out in alarm.

Cut the yarn about 6"/15cm from the hook. Draw the end of the yarn through the last loop on your hook. Pull the tail of the yarn gently to tighten the loop. This will prevent the accidental unraveling of your stitches.

Weaving in the End(s)

Thread a large-eyed tapestry needle with the tail of your yarn end. Weave the yarn through three or four stitches. To secure the weaving, weave back through the same stitches. Cut the yarn close to—but not up against—the crocheted fabric. Gently pull the fabric, and the yarn end will disappear into the stitches.

Weave in other yarn ends that you have on the wrong side of your fabric in the same way.

Blocking

As you crochet your poncho or pieces of your poncho may become a little misshapen. They may not look like perfect rectangles, precisely match the dimensions of the poncho, or the edges may be curled. With very few tools and a little effort, you can block an item to the shape that is desired or needed.

First and foremost, you'll need a flat, padded surface to work on. Some good choices: an ironing board, a mattress in the guest room, or a large piece of heavy cardboard slipped inside a large plastic trash bag. The size of your project will dictate the size of padded surface you need. Cover any flat surface with a sheet of plastic or a large trash bag to prevent moisture from damaging the surface. If needed, use a stack of several absorbent bath towels to pad your flat surface. You'll need the padding in order to stick pins into the padded surface to hold your work.

In addition to a flat surface to work on, you'll need the following simple tools to steam or spray block an item:

Rust-proof T-pins or straight pins
Steam iron
Spray bottle
Tape measure or ruler

Steam Blocking

Steam blocking is used to lightly block an item that has curling edges or one that is slightly misshapen.

1. Set your iron to a temperature that is compatible with the fiber content of your yarn. If in doubt about the fiber content, use a medium-low setting.

2. Lay your item flat on a padded surface. Lightly tug at the item to bring it into the shape desired. Use pins to hold the item to the desired shape on the padded surface. Check your measurements with a tape measure if needed.

3. Hold your heated steam iron about an inch above the fabric and steam the item. Never press the iron on the fabric!

4. Allow the item to cool and dry completely before removing the pins.

Spray Blocking

Spray blocking is a little more time-consuming than steam blocking (it takes longer to dry). It's useful if your item is more than a bit misshapen.

1. Lay your item flat on a moisture-protected, padded surface.

2. Gently stretch your item to conform to the correct shape or measurements. Pin the item in place with rust-proof pins.

3. Fill a clean spray bottle with lukewarm water. Spritz the item until it is slightly damp; don't soak it.

4. Smooth the fabric with your hands and pin it with additional pins if the edges are wavy.

5. Allow the crocheted item to dry completely before you remove the pins.

Putting It All Together

In the pattern directions each designer has specified the method used to assemble the garment. You may already have a preference for a specific assembling technique that you like. If you do, use it. Whatever technique you use, take time and care to put as much effort into assembling the poncho as you did making the individual pieces.

Whipstitch

With right sides together, neatly sew through both pieces from back to front through a strand—usually the top loops of a chain—on each piece. Leave a tail of about 6 inches (15 cm) hanging free, and weave in the yarn end after you've finished the seam. Take care to match stitches and rows.

Backstitch

Backstitching creates a sturdy seam. With right sides together, insert the needle from front to back at the seam edge, and then bring it from back to front a half-stitch space forward at 1. Insert the needle back where the stitch began at 2, and bring the needle forward at 3 (figure 64).

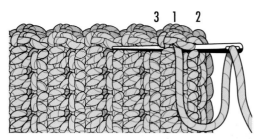

figure 64

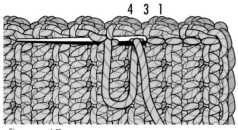

figure 65

Insert the needle a half stitch back from the yarn at 1 and up again a whole stitch forward at (figure 65). Work your way across the seam. Weave the yarn end in at the end of the seam.

Weaving

With the right sides of both pieces facing you, match the edges stitch for stitch. Sew through both pieces to secure the yarn, and leave a tail to weave in when you finish the seam.

Insert the needle from right to left through one strand on each piece. Bring the needle around and insert it again, from right to left, through the strands (figure 66). Continue to work in this way, tightening the seam edges as you work.

Slip Stitching

Using a crochet hook and yarn to join pieces is a neat method of working. If you work on the wrong side of the piece, a strong seam results. If you work on the right side of a piece, a decorative, embroidered stitch results.

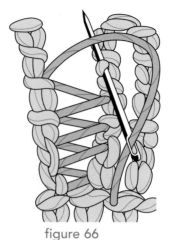

figure 66

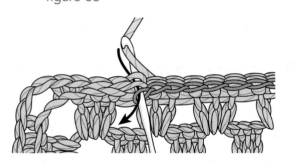

figure 67

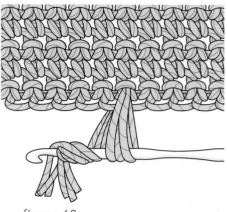

figure 68

1. Position two pieces together as directed, with right or wrong sides facing. Take care to be sure that the stitches match across the edge.

2. Work through both pieces using the same size crochet hook you used to crochet the pieces. Insert the hook through the back two loops of the first two stitches. Leave a yarn tail.

3. Yarn over, pull the yarn through. Repeat the stitch in each stitch along the seam. Weave in the yarn ends when you have stitched along the entire seam (figure 67).

Fringe

Fringe is an easy embellishment to add to any crocheted project you wish. Most patterns include specific directions for fringing your project, but if the urge to add a little fringe to a project that has none strikes you, here's a fool-proof method to use.

Cut a piece of cardboard approximately 4 inches (10 cm) wide and at least ½ inch (1 cm) longer than you want your finished fringe to be. Evenly wind your yarn around the cardboard until it is filled, then cut across one end. Set the cut lengths to one side. Continue winding and cutting as needed.

Pick up any number of strands and fold them in half. Working on the wrong side of the fabric, pull the folded end up through a stitch or space and pull the loose ends through the folded end (figure 68). Tighten the knot you've made. Continue working across the edge of the fabric, spacing the fringe as desired. For a neat finish, lay the fringed fabric on a hard surface and trim the yarn ends evenly.

Abbreviations

alt	alternate
Alt lp st	alternate loop stitch
approx	approximately
beg	begin, beginning
bet	betwee
BL	back loop
BP	back post
ch	chain
ch-sp	chain space
cont	continue
dc	double crochet
dec	decrease(s/ing)
dtr	double treble crochet
ea	each
esc	extended single crochet
FL	front loop
FP	front post
hdc	half double crochet
hk	hook
inc	increase(s/ing)
lp(s)	loop(s
oz	ounce(s)
patt	pattern
prev	previous
rem	remaining
rep	repeat
reverse sc	reverse single crochet
RS	right side
rnd(s)	round(s)
sc	single crochet
sk	skip
sl st	slip stitch
sp(s)	space(s)

st(s)	stitch(es)
tch	turning chain
tog	together
tr	treble croche
Tss	Tunisian simple stitch
Tsl	Tunisian slip stitch
Tks	Tunisian knit stitch
Tps	Tunisian purl stitch
WS	wrong side
V-st	V- stitch
yo	yarn over

Crochet Hook Sizes

Continental	U.S.
2.25 mm	B-1
2.75 mm	C-2
3.25 mm	D-3
3.5 mm	E-4
3.75 mm	F-5
4 mm	G-6
4.5 mm	7
5 mm	H-8
5.5 mm	I-9
6 mm	J-10
6.5 mm	K-10 1/2
8 mm	L-11
9 mm	M/N-13
10 mm	N/P-15
15 mm	P/Q
16 mm	Q
19 mm	S

*Letter or number may vary by manufacturer. For accurate and consistent sizing, rely on the millimeter (mm) size.

designer biographies

Linda Buckner is an award-winning fiber artist from Wheaton, Illinois. She uses high quality fibers in luscious colors, felt, fabric, antique embellishments, wire and more to create visually stunning art to wear, collages, home décor, and gift items. She creates new products for a toy manufacturer, teaches, and exhibits mixed media art nationally.

Joan Davis is one of the founding members of the Crochet Guild of America (CGOA). She is an accomplished and respected instructor in schools and at conferences around the country. She resides in Palm Beach County, Florida, with her cat, Opportunity.

Laura Gebhardt is a retired business executive. She began designin͏ ͏ ͏1996. Since then, more th͏ ͏ ͏ ͏in magazines, books, ͏ ͏ ͏crochet classes ͏ ͏ith an ever-increasi͏ ͏and and cat) near To͏

Donna͏ ͏ng in beautiful North ͏ ͏Retriever. She has be͏ ͏er life and learne͏ ͏rl. She is grateful to͏ ͏e taught, inspir͏

A life͏ ͏Power Johnson desig͏ ͏and crocheting. She's ͏ ͏er to push the creat͏ ͏articles have appe͏ ͏Knitting, Interwea͏ ͏es. She is the autho͏ ͏N Publishing, 2001). Kathleen teaches at many major needlework events, as well as for guilds and shops around the country.

Kalpna Kapoor has been crocheting since she was 10 years old. She teaches both knitting and crochet workshops. She owns Craft-Creations Knitting Studios in Newhall, California. This full-service retail store offers a full range of knitting and crochet classes, as well as a wide selection of fine yarns from around the world.

Robyn Kelly lives in Ventura, California. Her sister Amber, her nieces, and her goddaughter are the inspirations for (and recipients of!) her creative crochet. Like many others her grandmother taught her to crochet at an early age, but she considers herself self-taught.

Katherine Lee is a Los Angeles-based designer. Her innovative designs have been published in many magazines and books, and purchased via her web site by thousands of crocheters and knitters. She holds a degree in engineering and an MBA, but decided to combine her love of knitting and crochet into a full-time endeavor in 2001 by starting SweaterBabe.com

Jenny King is an Australian crocheter, designer and teacher. She travels regularly to the USA to teach at CGOA conferences. Many of her patterns have appeared in Crochet! Inspired by her tropical home, Jenny's designs are usually colorful and dramatic. At age 10, Jenny crocheted a cowl necked poncho composed of four granny squares. It's fitting that her newest ponchos appear in this book 36 years later.

Donna May is a self-taught crochet veteran of more than 40 years. For the past 20 years, she has been a hands-on healer and consulting astrologer as well. Though these disciplines may sound miles apart from crochet design, Donna will tell you they are more similar than different. She believes each is about patterns, cycles, creativity, and harmony. Inspired by her grandchildren, Donna is currently developing a line of crochet patterns for infants and children.

Marty Miller lives and teaches in Greensboro, North Carolina. She has been crocheting and creating her own patterns since she was a little girl. Her designs have appeared in magazines, books, and fashion shows, and in the pattern collections of a major yarn company. She is a professional member and the Mentor Coordinator of CGOA. When she is not crocheting or designing, Marty is a group exercise instructor and personal trainer at a local health club.

Willena Nanton has been crocheting for 28 years. She's currently the president of the New York City Crochet Guild and a member of CGOA. She's taught a variety of crochet classes and started a program for middle school students who stitched and donated blankets for babies in homeless shelters. Her designs have appeared in Today's Crochet Sweaters from CGOA (2003) and in Donna Kooler's Crocheted Afghans (2004).

Dora Ohrenstein began crocheting during the dawning of the Age of Aquarius, while living on a houseboat in Amsterdam. She then put crochet aside to pursue a career as a singer for the next 30 years, enjoying considerable success in classical music, touring all over the globe and making many recordings. In the summer of 2003, the hook called to her again, and she began designing crochet fashions, first for herself and subsequently for publication. She lives and works in Manhattan, where she continues to perform as well as teach singing at several local colleges. Balls of yarn cover much of the square footage of her studio apartment.

Freddie Schuh first learned to crochet doilies at age 10. Later, as a young mother, she tried to make a sweater, but it was "the stiffest thing I ever made" and she vowed never to crochet a garment again. She later joined *CGOA* and quickly became hooked on crochet once more. Now she designs and markets her own original patterns, as well as runs her city's first local yarn store.

Nanette Seale decided to try her hand at designing her own pattern while crocheting a baby sweater for her third child. Crochet is one of her favorite activities, but she also does cross-stitch and plastic canvas work. She has three sons and one married daughter.

Dee Stanzio lives in rural Connecticut with her husband and two young children. She's a Craft Yarn Council Certified Crochet Teacher. No stranger to winning blue ribbons for her work, Dee's Sweet Baby Afghan Sampler can be found in *Blue Ribbon Afghans from America's State Fairs: 40 Prize-Winning Crocheted Designs (Lark, 2004).*

Index